FINDING LOVE ON THE CAMINO

A MEMOIR

by Deborah Wilson

Table of Contents

Introduction 5

Chapter 1 On The Gucci Camino 9

Chapter 2 Pleased To Meet You, Boris 17

Chapter 3 The (Im)Perfect Pilgrim............................. 25

Chapter 4 Paradise Found 33

Chapter 5 Stuff The Squirrel! 43

Chapter 6 The Tilley Hat 53

Chapter 7 No Room At The Inn................................. 61

Chapter 8 Txirimiri 69

Chapter 9 Tent City.. 81

Chapter 10 The Singing Tree 87

Chapter 11 Blah, Blah. Blah 95

Chapter 12 The Fork In The Road 107

Chapter 13 The End Of The Road 117

Chapter 14 Monday Night Fever............................. 121

Chapter 15 The Crying Time 127

Chapter 16 The Long Hard Look 135

Chapter 17 Going For Gold...................................... 143

Chapter 18 The People Pleaser 147

Chapter 19 Lovely Luarca....................................... 155

Chapter 20 Armed And Angry 163

Chapter 21 The Songs Of Galicia 169

Chapter 22 Riding A Star 175

Chapter 23 Just Me.. 185

Chapter 24 Pulpo Feria Revisited 193

Chapter 25 Bursting The Balloon 201

Chapter 26 Norte No More.. 207

Chapter 27 Sadly Santiago.. 219

Chapter 28 The Last Supper.. 225

Chapter 29 And Then There Was One............................... 233

Epilogue.. 243

Introduction

This book is so very different from the one I had originally envisaged writing. I had a plan, a good plan, to collect all the wonderful stories of people falling in love on the Camino de Santiago. I was going to document those stories.

What happened to that plan?

I walked the Camino, and the Camino had another plan for me. It never even crossed my mind that I would one day have my own Camino story to tell…

For years, working as a guide on the Camino de Santiago, I had been fascinated by the stories of couples who had found each other whilst walking the Camino. What an incredible way to meet. Literally blessed by the stars on the path of the Milky Way. Any union starting under such auspicious circumstances could only be one of lifelong love and happiness. And when asked how they had met, it would sure beat saying 'on Tinder'. I couldn't imagine anything more romantic nor more joyous.

A close friend of mine, set off alone and met her very own Camino angel. With whom she now has two beautiful children. A lovely chap called, appropriately, Angel. Some years her junior, he from Granada and she from Buenos Aires, it was unlikely that their paths would ever cross. Only on the Camino could such miracles occur.

Another couple, he Australian, she British met whilst walking the Camino in 2015, neither of them in the first blush of youth. Their relationship blossomed, they got engaged, but were kept apart for twenty months during the pandemic. Their story went viral. He was finally granted special dispensation to leave Australia last October to fly to the UK to get married. Their reunion at Heathrow Airport was filmed by the BBC.

A German chap and a Spanish woman, both of them walking by themselves, had gone way off the main Camino trail and found themselves in a tiny, isolated chapel, believing themselves to be completely lost and alone. They instead literally bumped into the love of their life in that chapel. Last year they walked the Camino again to celebrate ten years of a gloriously happy marriage.

So, I thought I would write a book about these serendipitous meetings. Like a squirrel with her nuts, I started collecting these stories. But walking my own Camino put a stop to writing that book.

In 2017 my husband and I set out to finally walk our own Camino. We had been married and in a stable relationship for nineteen years. Our Camino was to be a heart-warming experience that would deepen our love for one another. However, my Camino did not follow that story line. It veered way off course, down a path so unexpected, so sad and so scary, I feared I might never find my way back.

I could never have imagined ending up with the version of the story that I now have to tell. In both the very worst and very best of ways.

No story like the previous ones mentioned. But it is my story, and I love it.

Walk with me and let me tell you my Camino story: 'Finding Love on the Camino'.

Chapter 1

ON THE GUCCI CAMINO

'Be curious not judgmental'

Walt Whitman

Spain? God. Why would anyone ever want to go there?! Asked my obnoxious 22 year old self. For me it represented ugly Brits grilling themselves lobster red and forming little Britain on the Costa del Sol. But, having signed up for a degree majoring in French, and given the choice of minoring in either German or Spanish, I reluctantly chose the latter. Neither held much appeal but at least the Spanish language did not have three genders to get to grips with. Two were more than enough, thank you very much.

And so, in the late 1980's, I found myself boarding a plane to Malaga for the first half of my obligatory year abroad. Stealing myself for the inevitable onslaught of tourist tat; sombrero wearing donkeys, flamenco dancer loo roll holders and Queen Victoria pubs, I grimly stepped off the plane. I can still absolutely remember exactly how the air smelt. My nose fairly quivered as I picked up the scent of something exotic and exciting, full of endless possibilities, and intensely vibrant and alive. As my bus rolled on towards Granada, my final destination, the endless olive groves, the hills and plains of Andalusia made their first assault on my senses. I wanted to poke my snoozing neighbours and ask them if they, also, saw what I was seeing. Or was I possibly dreaming? This enchanted landscape bore no resemblance whatsoever to the Spain of my English preconceptions. Not even the faintest whiff of cheap beer or fish n'chips.

When that bus crested the brow of a hill and the Sierra Nevada mountains loomed up towards me, I was forever hopelessly and utterly bewitched by Spain, this land of olives and wine. My neck got sore from swivelling to get a better view. I recognised myself in this landscape, it spoke to me. It absolutely rocked my soul. And that has never changed. As a linguist I have lived and worked in many other countries, but I have always considered Spain my home and the place of my highest joy.

My language skills later landed me a job as supervisor for an educational travel company that sent groups of US high school students to Europe. Not an easy job. I was constantly trouble shooting crazy situations across the continent such as missed flights for 45 people, national train strikes, buses breaking down, students falling out of hotel windows, students held in pending cells at the airport due to incorrect visas. On call 24/7 for 5 months of the year. The rest of my year? I had a second job. I was a tour guide on the Camino de Santiago.

Now if you don't know what the Camino de Santiago is let me fill you in. It is a pilgrimage trail or, more correctly, trails. The most famous is the Camino Frances. It measures 800 kms from a small town just the other side of the French border, called St Jean Pied de Port to its official end point, Santiago de Compostela, in the far west of Spain. Besides the Camino Frances, there are many other Camino trails to choose from. Centuries ago, the idea was to walk out of your front door to an established Camino trail and then follow it all the way to its end. Pilgrims throughout history have done just that. In the old days you did it to have your sins pardoned. You could even have them pardoned by proxy, paying someone else to walk it for you. Today, when you make it to Santiago, you can apply for a shiny, swirly certificate that states that you have "devoutly visited this most holy temple for reasons of piety". This part of the Camino experience, the religious aspect, has never appealed to me. I've never felt that religion need come into the picture. For me, living now in this century, walking a Camino must surely be about having a deeply personal, transformative experience.

I loved guiding the Camino tours. Our clients were mainly North American retirees. They were well heeled, from illustrious careers; lawyers, doctors, professors. Most had been inspired to don their walking boots by the movie 'The Way' with Martin Sheen. That movie had catapulted the Camino to fame in 2010. They had caught the Camino bug, but not badly enough to want to walk it alone as pilgrims, or stay in albergues, the cheap pilgrims' hostel accommodation you find all along the trail. They wanted the Camino experience without having the "real" experience. They wanted a pleasant walk through northern Spain with 5-star luxury always available to them. Or, as one of our clients dubbed it, the Gucci Camino experience. If the name fits …. and it did. It was my job, along with 2 other guides, to provide that 5-star Gucci Camino experience.

Finding Love On The Camino

I was not only tour guide and interpreter but host, raconteur, confidante, appeaser and cheer leader. I always had a long to-do list. Clients' needs, dietary and otherwise, were becoming more and more complex. I had to double and then triple check that our dinner menus were in accordance with their convoluted dietary requirements. Some clients were even allergic to wifi! Apparently, it's a thing. I honestly nearly burst out laughing when I was first told. Thankfully, for once, I held it in. As the appeaser, I assured the lady that the hotels we stayed in would be only too happy to give her a room that the wifi signal didn't reach. She was very appreciative. She slept soundly and that meant she was able to enjoy herself.

I always felt that my job, first and foremost most, was to make sure that everyone was happy. That was easy for me. I genuinely enjoyed making them happy. I laid out their gourmet picnics in perfect scenic surroundings. I thought up little ways to surprise and delight every client. Their favourite chocolate they happened to mention to me in passing. A woolly hat when I could see they were getting chilly. A set of compeed blister plasters for when I saw they were foot sore. I happily ran back kilometres to find things they had left behind, sunglasses, gloves, walking poles, their favourite water bottle… the list goes on.

At the end of each tour, we took the obligatory group photo in front of the cathedral in Santiago. They were dressed in their neatly pressed high end walking togs. Their faces slightly chubbier than when they had started out with us. There were no backpacks in the photo of course. They never had to carry one. As soon as the snap was taken, they photoshopped, facebooked and instagrammed that photo out to the world. It was evidence of one more item having been ticked off their bucket list. Their happiness was evident but, to my way of thinking, it was easily contained within the parameters of that photo. Their minds were already moving on to the next item on their list. When I look closely at those photos, I can see that all are smiling, looking into the camera. All except for me. My gaze is averted to one side, observing with forensic attention the real pilgrims. The stinky, sweaty, backpacked pilgrims who are taking their last steps as they arrive into the cathedral square. Their eruption of joy. That joy couldn't be contained within the parameters of any photo. I longed to know exactly how that felt. I yearned to experience the Camino as a real pilgrim and not as a tour guide.

Walking ON the Camino and being around pilgrims just wasn't doing it for me. I wanted that deeply transformative experience that I felt the Camino had to offer me. I realised that this transformative experience wasn't passed on through osmosis. I was only getting a superficial skimming of the surface. Nothing deeper. So why hadn't I gone off and walked the Camino myself? Simple. There was never enough time or enough money. My two jobs were back to back. When one finished the other started up again. Don't get me wrong, I staunchly defended the right of all to walk the Camino as they saw fit. I used to laugh along with my Gucci clients at the very idea of 'slumming it'. Why on earth would anyone choose to go back to their student days of eeking out a paltry budget and putting up with basic conditions? Why would anyone willingly regress when they could see the same places, witness the same beauty, enjoy exactly the same experience in comfort rather than in self-imposed penury? What sense did that make?

But I had a nagging little voice inside my head reminding me that the experience we were providing, wonderful as it was, was not the real

Finding Love On The Camino

Camino experience. I suspected that the whole point of being on the Camino was to step outside comfort zones. It wasn't just about the physical component parts of the journey. It was about doing things differently to how you had always done them. What would the Camino reveal to you if you put on a backpack, took a risk and walked without a guide like me having your back? But who was I kidding? Our clients were perfectly happy with the Gucci version. They had gorgeous accommodation. Dinner was always a gourmet four-course meal with matching wines, and then, I would lead them to the bar for after dinner drinks.

I remember the night it hit me that the only one I was short changing on these tours was myself. We were in the bar of a parador. Paradors are 5-star luxury hotels that you find in Spain. They are often renovated monasteries, castles and even palaces. I was surprised to see "real" pilgrims in the bar. The sort that actually walked the Camino all the way. I always thought an invisible force-field separated us from them. But there they were at the table next to us. They had muddy boots and dirty socks and gaunt faces to prove it. They were tired and grubby and sat comparing their war wounds as they went over the highs and the lows of their day. Every now and then one of them would fling their arms up in the air in spontaneous outbreaks of rapturous joy. They were impervious to the disgusted looks from the barman. A little drunk, they were enveloped in a warm glow that I could only put down to being in the middle of that real Camino experience. God, I wanted to be one of them. I wanted to have muddy boots too. I wanted to get a little stinky. I wanted to rinse out my smalls in freezing water. In a nano second, I would have traded my fluffy bath robe and slippers waiting for me upstairs, with a handkerchief sized travel towel and a pair of flip flops. Maybe I could even have a bunk next to a fat, farting German. Damn it. I wanted in on the real Camino deal. That night I knew in my heart that something was about to give. I was unhappy just being on the Camino without knowing what that "real" Camino experience was like.

****

That Gucci Camino season came to an end. No more making polite, small talk with clients, no more laying out picnics in picturesque spots, or schlepping monogrammed suitcases to 5-star rooms No more juggling of other people's needs and wants. No checking off "to do" lists while the gorgeous Spanish countryside passed me by unnoticed.

We returned to our home in Granada, drained and depleted. 'We' being Pedro, my Argentinian husband and I. He sometimes worked alongside me as a Gucci Camino tour guide. He was understated, intelligent, highly practical and informed. People gravitated to his air of calm, quiet authority. He was a lawyer in Argentina but his qualifications, sadly, were unrecognised in Spain. He was unwilling to begin another seven years of study. It had been a tortuous process doing it the first time around and, as he would always say, he wasn't up for a second bout in the ring.

Our little home in Granada was a cave house. Two bedrooms were actually dug out of the chalky hills. In my student days it was a bar. I remember spending far too much time there. Time that should have been spent in the library studying. When they were renovating, they found a skeleton of a donkey standing upright. Poor old Eyeore. This was a very quirky and charming home. And it was bloody cheap.

Finding Love On The Camino

Pedro pointed out that, with the money we were saving on rent, we could now get by without the Gucci Camino gig. The thought had not occurred to me. Holy crap. He was right. Then he said something earth shattering. "And now you and I can walk our own Camino, Kiki." I was stunned. I had no words. I heard angels singing. Oh my God, why not indeed? Nothing was now stopping me from having that Camino experience for myself. I could sign on the dotted line for a pilgrim passport. Pedro and I could actually go and be one of THEM. We could take our place in the sweaty, grubby ranks of the real pilgrims. Oh my God. I bounced Tigger-like off our cave walls. I loved him, he was a genius. I could see the Camino yellow arrows, the ones that the pilgrims follow on their way to Santiago de Compostela, pulsating around the room. Which arrows would we follow?

Chapter 2
PLEASED TO MEET YOU, BORIS

"If you're not excited about it, it's not the right path."

Abraham Hicks

Which Camino would we walk? There are, arguably, seven main routes of the Camino de Santiago, and a complicated array of offshoots as well. Definitely not the Camino Frances. Although, for many, this is THE Camino. For us it was inextricably linked with work. We wanted something new, a fresh challenge.

We thought about the Portuguese Camino, from Lisbon to Santiago de Compostela. We had already walked the rural inland route with groups, so that was out. We considered walking the coastal variant, a series of boardwalks and beaches with the Atlantic Ocean tumbling to our left. Sounded lovely. I always find being by the ocean the most uplifting place in the world. But the walk itself didn't feel like a challenge.

Finding Love On The Camino

We could be like the pilgrims of old and walk from our home. We had the Mozarabe route literally on our doorstep. The name Mozarabe refers to the Christians who were allowed to live here and practise their own religion when Granada was under Muslim rule, until the reconquest by the so called 'Catholic Kings' Ferdinand and Isabel in 1492. Or we could start on the Costa del Sol in Malaga or from the south-eastern city of Almeria. We could follow the Roman Via Augusta path, passing through the Moorish delights of Cordoba and the Roman remains of Merida joining up with the Camino de la Plata, coming from Seville. But having lived in Andalusia for many years we wanted something new.

We turned our attention northwards. Some say the Camino del Norte is the most beautiful of all the Caminos. It is a less crowded and totally new to us. It is just over 800 kms long. There is some debate as to its 'official' starting point. Some say that it is across the French border in St Jean de Luz most maintain that it starts in the bustling city of Irun on the French/Spanish border. It takes in some of the most stunning coastal scenery, beautiful beaches, gorgeous inlets and estuaries, wide expanses of sand. Lots of off-road walking deep in forests and the fun challenge of roller coaster hills. Little gems of villages are dotted along the way to surprise and delight the weary pilgrim. And with two of my favourite cities in Spain; San Sebastián and Bilbao to look forward to. Also, we could hook up with the Camino Primitivo, the oldest Camino of them all. This route covers 320kms of very tough terrain, rugged and mountainous. It is both challenging and uniquely beautiful.

Pedro really wanted to tackle the Camino Primitivo. I think he wanted to prove he was up to walking what is known by many as the toughest Camino. But not me. I was in awe of its reputation. I was afraid of those steep hills. I was afraid of going up them. And then there was the coming down, the slippery descents. I convinced myself I could rise to the challenge. I was riding the slipstream of Pedro's excitement, determined to turn my feelings of anxiety into excitement too. It's good to be taken out of your comfort zone, right? What is that saying, there's no growth in comfort and no comfort in growth. Hell, any Christmas cracker affirmation that would help me get over myself and my fear of going up and coming down those hills. If he really wanted this challenge, then I was certainly not going to stand in his way. I was going to make sure it happened for him. I wanted him to have the best Camino experience.

So, at the end of August, we had made our decision. We were going to combine two Caminos. We would start in Irun on the French/Spanish border and walk the Camino del Norte until a turn off, just past the city of Gijon in the province of Asturias, that would connect us with the Camino Primitivo. And then, having taken that turn off we would walk the Camino Primitivo into Santiago de Compostela. The calendar was just about to click over into autumn. Early autumn was one of the very best times of year to walk the Camino. It is a time of gentle warmth, of cooler evenings. The sunflowers would still be out. The grape harvests would be in full swing. The leaves would be starting to change colour. We didn't need to begin training for our Camino. Pedro and I were both Camino fit from the many months we spent walking with the Gucci Camino groups.

Absolutely everything was lining up. It would be a shared challenge that could only bring us closer together. We would be relaxed, revitalised, full of Camino joy and love. And that could only strengthen our commitment and love for each other. Things had been a tad rocky between us at times. Pedro had the constant pressure of having little work and being financially dependent upon me. He loved our adopted country, Spain, as much as I did but, even so, he missed Argentina and his family too. It's not easy to remain positive and upbeat when you feel something is missing from your life. This Camino would mean the celebration of a new phase for us. New and exciting beginnings. It had come at the perfect time. I couldn't have been more stoked at the prospect of it all.

Next, we had to work out how to get from Granada to Irun, our start to the Camino del Norte. That should be easy, we thought. But it wasn't. The only viable option was a car share ride on the 2nd of September. That was five days away. Car sharing had become quite the thing in Spain. It was safe and simple. We had used it many times. But we couldn't possibly get ready in less than a week and, further complicating things, I had a compulsory work conference in Sarajevo on the 16th of September, ten days into this proposed Camino schedule. We tried everything to find a later departure date; train, plane, and bus, they were either stupidly expensive or stupidly unworkable. Or both. If we wanted to walk the Camino del Norte, we had to take that car share ride on the second.

What to do? We checked the car share app again. There were now only two spaces left in that car. At any moment they could be snapped up. I could see a rival couple packing their bags and taking our spaces in that car. We knew it would be touch and go whether we would be ready on time. We hadn't finished moving into our new cave home. We had cars to insure, business affairs to put in order, all the boring day to day stuff of life that we had put off, while on tour, was now coming against us. But we didn't want to miss this opportunity to walk the Camino, so we booked.

Blimey. SO much to be done. We entered a period of wild frenzied organisation. On our list of things to do were new backpacks. Ours were heavy and outdated. We had never actually had to carry them on our backs! On the Gucci Camino they rode in the luggage compartment of the bus. We went to a hiking store tucked down a side street. It housed a huge hidden basement filled with backpacks. We were sucked into its depths for several hours. A confusing array of sizes, colours, weights, frames or no frames, water systems and straps. It was overwhelming. One backpack at the bottom of the mountainous pile seemed to be winking at me. Or the eye of the eagle with which it was emblazoned was. On closer inspection I saw that it wasn't an eagle it was an osprey. I reached down to it and swung it onto my back. It felt comfortable. It felt light. It felt right. It felt like a friend. And it was purple. Before I could procrastinate, I turned my back on the other candidates and headed to the cash desk.

And so began my relationship with Boris, my backpack. It was to be an intense one. Friend and confidant. My constant companion through the Camino and beyond. I felt almost shy as we started to make ourselves known to each other on our first walk together from the town centre to home. He felt right, he felt dependable. Oh, and why Boris? Well, he was to be my constant companion on my Camino, like a substitute pet.

I longed for a dog. I always had. My professional life didn't allow for a dog. So, until it did, Boris the backpack would be my surrogate dog.

Finding Love On The Camino

Scoff all you like. Pleased to meet you, Boris. I have a feeling we're going to get on well.

Now I had two lots of packing to organise. Packing Boris for the Camino and packing a travel bag for the five days I would be at that work conference in Sarajevo. The Spanish Post Office had just introduced a backpack delivery service making it easier for pilgrims to get to their Camino starting point. I was the first person in Granada to test it out. But not with Boris. I sent my travel bag packed with my civilian clothes for the work conference. The desk clerk looked dubiously at my red Samsonite . I quickly pulled out its concealed straps, so it looked more like a backpack. He raised an eyebrow, but no objections, and dispatched my bag to the Bilbao Post Office.

Two days before we left something most unexpected happened. I got a call from my accountant saying that I had to update and confirm my legal status. In Spain, any legal procedure was done in triplicate. A labyrinth of legalese and paperwork involved. Not what I needed to hear right now. Pedro had a Spanish passport and I, as his British wife, had assumed I was legal. Seldom will you get a black or white answer to anything in Spain. Particularly legal questions. We had never been sure if I was fully legal or not. Probably. But possibly not. Probably wasn't a comfortable place to be in. I was running the risk of being heavily fined or even worse, deported. The only way to rectify this was for me to bite the bullet and pay the ghastly fees associated with registering as self-employed. Straight into my accountant's office I went, no faffing about, paperwork signed. He said to leave it to him, he would file it all. Blimey. Was it really that simple? A few days later I was 'autonoma', self employed, no longer dependent on Pedro to continue living and working in Spain.

+++++++++

So, on the 2nd of September, as the summer break came to an end, Pedro and I stood on the side of the road waiting for our car share ride. Everyone around us was going back to school, or back to the office. I felt like a kid waiting for the bus on her first day of school. Uniformed and ready for action. Boris at my feet. I gave him a comforting pat on the head. Our car share ride, a white Peugeot 205 drew up. Carlos, the driver, greeted us warmly. He was relieved to see the size of our luggage. Our backpacks nestled contentedly into the boot. With three passengers in the back, it was a snug fit all round. We were on our way.

Carlos was a fast but safe driver. We hurtled northwards. In the rear-view mirror, the Sierra Nevada mountains grew smaller. We swept up and across the Meseta, the windmill country of Don Quixote. We left the metropolis of Madrid behind. The familiar names of the Camino Frances, Burgos, Atapuerca, came and went. We munched on our picnic lunches in the car. I was too excited to eat much. We stopped only for petrol and coffee. We were all intent on arriving in Irun as soon as possible. We had an entire Camino's length journey of over 800 kms to cover. We would be arriving early evening. At this time of year, even on a Friday, the municipal albergue, our accommodation for the night, would not be crowded - municipal albergues are public, as opposed to private albergues, generally owned and operated by the local government. There would probably be some Spaniards there, out on a weekend hike. We didn't foresee a problem.

The first Camino del Norte names appeared; Zumaya, Askizu, Zarautz. The tongue twisting Basque names, exotic and thrilling. To this day the origins of the Basque language, Euskera, remain unknown. The Basque Country is homeland to the Basque people, straddling the border of Spain and France. They have a long and convoluted history; from the 19th century on, a faction of them have been seeking their independence from the Spanish State. We turned right towards Irun in a reverse Camino. Carlos deposited us by an unimposing building that was the Irun municipal albergue. Its facade proudly proclaimed its status as the official home of the pilgrim. They buzzed us in.

Chapter 3
THE (IM)PERFECT PILGRIM

"Ring the bells that still can ring

Forget your perfect offering

There is a crack in everything

That's how light gets in."

Leonard Cohen

Inside the albergue, we excitedly filled in our pilgrim passports. Only pilgrims with an official pilgrim passport can stay in pilgrim albergues. Tonight, we would sleep as pilgrims in a bunk bed in a shared dormitory. We signed the register. We dropped the small fee, 10€, into the box. Hooray! We were officially pilgrims. We had our sleeping bags ready to claim our bunk, as pilgrims do.

The place was buzzing. Much more so than we had expected. Many were Spaniards. Some just on a weekend Camino jaunt. Some taking advantage of the tail end of their summer break. Some just starting out on their own full-blown Camino. The latter were mainly small groups of retired middle-aged men. Indistinguishable from each other in their grey walking togs. But there were also Russians, French, Italians, Americans and Brits and a smattering of other nationalities thrown into the mix.

Folk in varying stages of undress milled around us. The place was basic but clean. All the bunks we could see had sleeping bags on them. We had been assured of a bed, but where? The dour, direct Basque chap in charge told us to follow him. We passed more rooms housing about 15 pilgrims each. The place looked to be a repurposed school. But surely there were only so many classrooms. Pedro and I trotted behind him exchanging worried glances. We went down a few flights of stairs glimpsing more of the same, to either side of the corridors. My head swivelling from side to side. I spotted no unclaimed bunks as we passed.

He took us down the last remaining flight of stairs. We seemed to be heading for the street. That was odd. We turned left out of the main door and went down a slope into what looked like a garage. It was a garage! Housing the overspill. Which, he told us, that night was going to be 60 pilgrims. Correction. 62 with us. As he showed us into the garage his expression was one of contempt. Apparently this albergue had been after bigger premises for some time. He stood with us, shaking his head, surveying the scene before us.

I glanced at Pedro who was trying to look appreciative. He wasn't doing too well. Bunks pressed up against each other were separated by what looked like cardboard. There was only room for one person at a time to stand between them. People bumped into each other in a confusion of apologies. One bare light bulb swung from the ceiling. No natural light entered down here. I could see four remaining empty spaces. Perfect. We had a bed. My rose-tinted glasses were firmly in place. "It's great!" I trilled. And actually, meant it. It could have been a chicken coop for all I cared. The Basque chap turned to me, shocked. This was obviously not the reaction he had expected. "No, it's not." He spat. "It's shit."

We snagged the bunks opposite a rather sombre middle aged French couple who nodded their greetings. There wasn't room to reach out for a handshake. Backpacks stowed, sleeping bags in place, we headed out to find something to eat. Despite our late arrival, we were in no danger of missing out on dinner, most restaurants in Spain don't open until 8pm. However municipal albergues have a strict curfew time to ensure a good night's sleep for their pilgrims. We had to make it back under the tripwire before 10pm. Which suited me just fine. Pedro, being a night owl, was not so thrilled at the news.

We jumped on a bus to the neighbouring village of Hondarribia, just a 5 km hop away, sitting on the bay opposite the French town of Hendaye just across the water. We could have hoofed it there, but time was of the essence. Hondarribia was buzzing with activity and excitement, kicking off proceedings for the festival of their patron saint the Virgin of Guadalupe this weekend. Which explained the number of Spaniards in the albergue. They were here to both join in the fun and take a short jaunt on the Camino.

Spaniards love an excuse to party. And in the Basque Country, any local festivity is an opportunity to parade their deep pride in their heritage. The town was dressed to the nines. Like kids whose doting parents had spent hours preparing their offspring for an important social gathering, crucial that they should be squeaky clean and impeccably presented. Every building had been lovingly bathed, primped and pressed, decked out in all its finery. The final tweaks were being made; hankies whipped out of pockets and spat on to rub off last minute grubby marks, hair done up in brightly coloured ribbons, shoes polished to such a shine they reflected wide-eyed excited faces.

Every twist and turn we took around the winding streets revealed more brightly flowered, flag festooned balconies. The facades of the houses were multi-coloured and jostling for space under their A-framed roofs. Some streets were so narrow that neighbours could step on to their balconies and reach out and shake hands with those opposite. Tall skinny homes competed for space with their more corpulent neighbours, holding their breath, squeezed in between them. All the locals were dressed in red and white, mostly red berets & scarves, white shirts & trousers. Or some combination of the above. Dressed in our soberly coloured walking gear we stood out as obvious outsiders. But I didn't care at all. Because we were pilgrim outsiders, we had our own identity of which to be proud.

In the more central arcaded plazas space was at a premium. And belonged rightfully to the locals. We found a bar in a quiet back street and ordered wine and tapas, or rather pintxos as they are known in the Basque Country and toasted the start of our Camino. Pintxos are delicacies often served on small pieces of bread held together with cocktail sticks. We had cured ham, chorizo sausage, olives, local cheeses and tortilla. They hit the spot. I've always loved the tapas/pintxos culture. You don't have to commit to a full-blown meal but get to sample a selection of all that is delicious in the area.

Things were really hotting up as we prepared to head back to the albergue due to our 10pm curfew. Bands tuned up and took a turn around their marching route. Skittish horses pranced in circles. Fireworks seemed to spontaneously combust unable to contain themselves. Pedro had a severe case of FOMO, fear of missing out. Whereas I was so focused on the personal party we had in store, all the thrills and adventure of a Camino ahead of us, far more thrilling a prospect than a night of boozy revelry. I felt Pedro's frustration. He would have loved to have stayed out with the locals until the wee hours. But we had to get back to our garage. We made it back, just in time. Boris looked relieved to see me.

I experienced an irrepressible fit of the giggles as I texted with my sister Penny. I sent her photos of our garage. She was appalled. Her reaction only made me laugh even more. The more horrified she got, the funnier it seemed to me. And I couldn't stop. I just couldn't see it through her eyes. Nothing could burst my Camino bubble. The serious French couple opposite me seemed alarmed to be sleeping opposite a possibly unhinged laughing woman.

I expected to be kept awake by a symphony of snoring and other bodily eruptions detailed at great length in Camino chatrooms. So, I put in my ear plugs and cocooned myself, snug as a bug, in my sleeping bag. I fell asleep reconnecting with a feeling of joy and fun I so clearly remember having as a child. The next thing I heard was the 5am, pre-dawn stirrings of sixty sleep befuddled pilgrims rustling through their backpacks for toothbrushes and socks. Most of us were not yet skilled in the art of retrieving much needed items from our packs without making a right old palaver of it. It was the albergue dawn chorus! I lay there with a stupid grin on my face and enjoyed it.

Finding Love On The Camino

I was thinking about the fun I was going to have seeing the Camino with new eyes. I was going to see it from a "real pilgrim" perspective. But I wasn't going to fall into the trap of the pilgrim syndrome of blind introspection that I had witnessed many, many, many, many times on the Camino. This syndrome causes pilgrims to be oblivious to the fact that they are marching right through the heart of the everyday lives of the Spanish people. I wanted to be the very best pilgrim I could be. I wanted to tread lightly. No pre-dawn hammering of feet and walking poles for me. No talking at top volume as I walked past people's front doors, especially as most Spaniards don't go to bed until past midnight. No miscalculating my backpack dimensions and taking out unsuspecting locals. No falling into the trap of judging my fellow pilgrims. No wimping out and taking buses or taxis. I was going to be an A+pilgrim.

I was jerked out of this reverie at 6am when the beam of the lone swinging light bulb snapped on. With just the two loos separated by shaky plywood, and no ventilation, no one was tempted to linger. We all feigned deafness to the sounds of bodily functions usually only heard by those nearest and dearest to us. I shall avoid mentioning the olfactory implications, you really don't need to experience that, even vicariously. Hot showers were reserved for those with main albergue privileges. There was no hot water left for us garage dwellers. A frenzy of activity followed. The stampede for the door was intense. Judging by the ill-tempered mutterings not all had appreciated the night's accommodation as I had. The dedicated team of Camino volunteers, hospitaleros, had tried to make it the best they could. It was warm, it was dead cheap, and the best part as far as I was concerned was that we were welcomed as "real" pilgrims. Obviously, not all considered being a pilgrim a privilege as I did.

Before we began walking our Camino, we needed coffee. In a Spanish city you're always close to a bar. The challenge can be to find a bar that keeps pilgrim hours. Our fellow garage inmates, en masse, invaded the bars closest to the albergue. We walked a few blocks more, talking softly, treading lightly, conscious of not getting in the way of the locals as they went about their business. Me, conscious of being the perfect A+pilgrim. The bar we chose was my favourite sort of bar. The slot machines chirped their welcome. Old men in flat caps drank their morning carajillo, coffee with a generous dash of brandy. Or brandy with a splash of coffee. The telly was on in the corner blaring out the morning news. All was wrapped in the enticing smell of strong coffee and warm tostadas. I loved it.

We hopped on to the bar stools, always our preferred position in a bar. I parked Boris next to my stool and headed straight for the loo while Pedro ordered the coffee. I had preferred to cross my legs and squeeze rather than brave the garage facilities. When I came out Boris was lying flat out on his back blocking everyone's way. A frail elderly lady was clambering unsteadily over him. I was horrified! I ran to help her, apologising profusely. "Lo siento mucho!", I'm so sorry in Spanish.

So, on my first bona fide pilgrim morning I had broken my most treasured of perfect pilgrim rules - no taking out the locals. I had to give myself a pilgrim D- for that. And I hadn't even begun walking yet.

Chapter 4
PARADISE FOUND

"I feel that we are all lighthouses, and my job is to shine my light as brightly as I can to the darkness"

Jim Carey

And just like that, without any farewell committee, no drum roll or fanfare we were off. Taking our first steps on the Camino del Norte. No longer observing it from the outside, we were in it and of it. We were pilgrims. We spotted our first yellow arrow, and our journey was all in front of us. That arrow was pointing us all the way to Santiago de Compostela, 800 or so kms away. We followed.

Shortly after our first yellow arrow we received our first "Buen Camino". It felt bloody great. "Buen Camino" is the universal greeting on the Camino. It translates as 'good path" or "good journey'. It can come to you from fellow pilgrims or from the local people as you pass them on the path. It was issued to us by a rather unkempt local chap who had obviously just rolled out of bed. He looked to be out on his morning constitutional. He had his golden Labrador trotting faithfully at his side. His "Buen Camino" was probably a throwaway remark as he contemplated his day ahead. I'm sure he automatically bestowed the same greeting countless times on countless mornings without giving it a second thought. Whereas I wanted to stop and shake his hand, ask him his name, take a photo with him to mark this momentous occasion. Fortunately, I restrained myself and let him pass on by on his way into his busy day. On the Gucci Camino when I received this greeting, I always felt a fraud as if I had received an unearned reward. But here, on the Camino del Norte, I stood savouring those four sweet syllables, rolling them around my mouth, "Buen Camino".

It was perfect walking weather, and it wasn't long before the bustling centre of Irun gave way to the outskirts, and the outskirts gave way to country lanes. We took our final look back down over Irun and Hondarribia, which would, very slowly, be waking up and nodding to its neighbour Hendaye just across the water in France. There would be a fair few sore heads in Hondarribia this morning and still a full weekend of partying ahead of them. I was so happy not to be amongst the hungover hordes. I was partying on, in my own fashion, on this beautiful camino morning.

We were rocking along now. A familiar sense of contentment settled over me. Nature is very much my home, always has been. I felt relaxed and deeply connected with everything around me. Clear skies were overhead, sun but not too much. It always took me a while to adjust to the slower pace of walking, having been a runner for many years. The trail wasn't busy but there was a steady stream of people. Pilgrim etiquette is to pass on the right. We made a bit of noise to alert the pilgrims or locals ahead, of our presence, and then, "Buen Camino – ing", we motored on past them. We were walking a mix of sandy trails, roads and woodland paths. I stopped to greet some miniature shaggy ponies, their gorgeous brown eyes looking out and up from under their long blonde manes. They looked in need of a good haircut. They tolerated but didn't invite my caresses. This might feel like a supremely special morning to me but to them I was nothing special. Pilgrims were two a penny around here. There was an abundance of farm stock, horses, cows, sheep all totally underwhelmed by our presence. No trotting over to wish us "Buen Camino".

Pedro and I walked with a sense of purpose. Me taking two paces to each one of his long-legged strides. After nineteen years together we slipped effortlessly into step with each other. We'd first met in a salsa bar in Cozumel, Mexico. He was there with his outgoing mate, Juan. I was much more interested in Pedro, the shy, unassuming friend. I sensed his timidity, so I orchestrated our first date. I invited him out with friends cycling around the island. On the day, the friends were 'unable to make it'! It was just the two of us. Just like it was now. We walked with focus, a touch of competition between us. Our eyes were already skilled in the art of yellow arrow detection. We could sense them at a hundred paces and were both keen to prove our superior skills. Spotting the ones lurking under branches, hidden behind wheelie bins, and the faded and weather-worn ones invisible to the less well-honed eye.

By mid-morning we had covered a respectable distance. We had seen our first chapels and hermitages, one of them dating from the 12th century, but we didn't linger to visit them. We were on a mission. We bounded up our first significant elevation before starting the descent towards Paisajes de San Juan. There we found a beautiful albergue, Santa Ana. I called the number posted on the door. The very helpful chap told me they didn't open until 4pm. It had only just turned eleven in the morning. What to do? We couldn't just hang around until they opened. There was another very nice private albergue, he said, called The Twelve Tribes about an hour or so away. They would be open. Why didn't we carry on to there? Pedro and I agreed to do that.

Down the hill we quick marched towards the ferry crossing at Paisajes de San Pedro. On the Camino del Norte you get to experience the full glory of expansive sea views. They disappear as you follow the twists and turns of the path only to greet you again around the next bend. You also get to hop on pilgrim approved, picture perfect ferry boats that carry you across the bays between the villages. They look like colourful toy tugboats. Such fun. And it's not cheating.

We sat on a cafe terrace, in contented contemplation of it all. The typical Basque sloping roofs, balconies and multicoloured facades looked like a film set in which we got to play the extras. Pedro had his second breakfast, a tostada, a lightly toasted baguette halved and slathered with olive oil. Don't knock it till you try it. Not that I could. No problem. I preferred to eat post-walking anyway. In our little Camino party of two I was the one with the dietary restrictions. I'm a proper celiac. No gluten for me. Never, ever! At dinner I always go for the ensalada mixta. It is a mixed salad that is a staple all over Spain. The perfect blend of fresh lettuce, tomatoes, olives, grated carrot, egg and tuna. That and tortilla, a delicious thick egg and potato omelette, are pretty much guaranteed to be available anywhere in Spain from lunchtime on. They're what fuelled me. And bananas. I always had a stash of bananas to power me through the day.

Onwards and upwards. A prolonged set of rough-hewn stone steps. We turned corners only to see more of the same. We both paused at the top to catch our breath and pretend it had been easy. It hadn't. My mind raced forward. I needed to be sure we had a bed for the night. I had promised myself to go with the flow and not get anxious over the details. But all my years of Gucci Camino problem solving was getting in my way. The Camino would provide I assured myself. I just had to stay present and trust. That intention lasted only a few minutes before I started worrying about that bed again. As we approached woods ahead, the signs were unclear. I did not want us to miss that albergue. It was my duty to problem solve. I called the helpful chap from the Santa Ana albergue again. He was a touch less warm this time. He said to turn right and continue past the lighthouse. So, we did. And after that, forest trails with sea views led us to a brightly coloured sign welcoming us to the Twelve Tribes albergue.

The Twelve Tribes albergue was a vision of loveliness. A rose lined path delivered us to our cake wielding, tea bearing hosts. We were greeted with warmth. They looked as if they had stepped out of an Amish community. The women wore long skirts and headscarves while the men were bearded and hatted. They had an air of purpose and quiet contentment. The Twelve Tribes is an organised religion that has a contentious reputation. What I can attest to is that they received us beautifully. Everything about this place was the polar opposite of our previous night's garage. A golden stone building, the comforting scent of freshly baked goods and lush well-tended gardens. We were shown to the pilgrims' dormitory under the eaves. It was spotless. In the showers were honey scented bars of soap. They smelled so delicious I had to resist taking a bite out of them. And lashings of hot water. Even a deluxe washing machine. We sat in quiet disbelief. We could actually stay here. I think our dour straight-talking Basque hospiatelero from Irun would have approved of this. It was dreamlike.

Our smalls laundered. Boris stowed. It was still early afternoon and dinner would not be until the usual Spanish hour of 8pm. Pedro and I decided to head back to take a closer look at the lighthouse. I love lighthouses. There is something inherently calming and magical about them. I feel soothed by their solid, comforting presence. Not even the wildest storm can deflect their constant beam of light reaching out to all, guiding them, letting them know that they are not alone. They are safe. As long as they focus on that unwavering shaft of light they will sail into calmer waters.

As we walked, I saw a lone figure, head bowed, trudging in our direction. As the pilgrim came closer, I could see it was a woman. A tall, statuesque, black woman. She was stooped with fatigue. I was immediately drawn to her. I tend to form instant attachments in a rather intense, overly eager puppy type fashion. I almost fell over my words in my eagerness to lure her to our albergue. She was calm and considered in her response, evidently knackered. Maybe we would see her there on our return. I so hoped we would.

Even the lighthouse was pepper pot perfect. The business end of it was built atop a squat square stone structure. Solid and impenetrable. Sadly, also impenetrable to us, it was 'strictly no entry'. I would have loved to get in and scamper up the steps for the view. Still, it was good to know that the location of our albergue meant that we would sleep within the radius of its sweeping beam. I touched its walls warmed by the early autumn sun and thanked it for watching over us. It reminded me of another time, another place and another lighthouse. Early in our relationship, Pedro and I had lived opposite the remains of a lighthouse on the island of Cozumel. In a lovely little rustic house on a tiny bay. With a palapa roof terrace, covered in palm fronds that quietly rustled as we sat beneath it, hand in hand, watching the sun setting. It had been a wonderful place to start a new life together.

On our return to our heavenly albergue more pilgrims had joined the ranks. I checked out the beautiful grounds, hands clasped behind my back admiring the roses and the fruiting fig trees. I love figs. And this time of year, early autumn, was prime time for them. The only blot on this magnificent landscape was the presence of a particularly obnoxious ex-military, thuggish type of Brit. I overheard him making unkind comments about big-arsed women walking the Camino. How mean spirited of him. He wasn't exactly svelte himself. Thank goodness he was camping out. No chance of bumping into him later in the dorm.

There were quite a few pilgrims camping out. A very fit couple had set up a tent in a beautiful spot next to the rose garden. I introduced myself to them and they, in turn, to me. Sarah and Richard were from Canada. He was cycling and she was walking the Camino. A Swedish guy was making a fuss. He didn't like the ginger nectar welcome drink he was offered. He wanted a coke. I had to check the urge that came over me to find him that coke. Not my job. I reminded myself. I'm a fellow pilgrim. There was no sign of the woman we had met on our afternoon walk. I went up to the dorm to check if she was there. I quietly opened the door. Someone was lying with their feet sticking out over the end of the bed. Their back was turned. It was definitely her. Happy, I quietly pulled the door to.

Next, I checked out the kitchen, perhaps I could help out. The women were welcoming though a touch reserved. As I chopped and diced, I asked about their community. They were gracious but not forthcoming. All I discovered was that they were a world-wide sect. There was no feeling that we would be force fed their religion with our dinner.

We took our places at the dining tables. Just my luck. I was seated next to the tattooed ex-military thug I had overheard in the garden. The one who was being judgemental about female pilgrims. Where did he get off? After all, he was short, bald, had a London accent, a swaggering air and that nasty tattoo. I sincerely hoped Pedro and I would not cross paths with him after this evening. Between Pedro and me was seated a quiet, gangly German youth called Steffen. He was very shy but seemed comfortable in Pedro's company. The woman we had met earlier on the trail entered the dining room. I eagerly gestured to her to sit in the chair opposite me. She looked surprised at my enthusiasm, but sat down. Great. She was someone I really wanted to hang out with. I could focus on her and ignore the tattooed Brit. Her name was Diola. She was Nigerian and had lived in Germany for many years. I loved her air of self-contained poise.

A Twelve Tribes community member was seated at each of the tables. Grace was said. The Brit, whose name was Andy, started to hold court as carafes of water were placed on the tables. The wine would surely follow. Plates of salad emerged from the kitchen. No wine. Evidently drinks were not included. I asked if I might buy a glass of wine. No, was the answer. It was paradise, but an alcohol-free paradise. No wine, no beer. The Brit's eyes met mine. He was as aghast as I was. In that moment we bonded.

I wolfed down my plate of salad. And accepted a second helping and a third, knowing that I wouldn't be eating the main course of pasta. Despite myself I started to find the Brit funny. Diola too exploded with laughter. Her face lit up. She visibly loosened. I had the impression it might have been a while since she had relaxed like this. Soon Andy had the whole table in uproar. Especially me. I could barely raise my knife and fork so weakened was I with laughter. He turned to me and said, "You haven't heard British humour in a while, have you?" He was spot on. I had no idea how much I'd missed laughing. My ribs hurt. Those muscles hadn't been exercised for a long time. It had felt so good to let go and laugh.

Dinner over and no bar to go to we retired to our dorm. At 4am I suddenly came to, wide awake. I was starving. Carb deprived. I tiptoed to the door and did my best to open it quietly, without waking anyone. I made my way to the garden. I was set on foraging for those figs I had seen that afternoon. The Brit had his hammock tied to the only fig tree with branches low enough for me to reach. Darn it. I didn't want to wake him. I did my best to plunder in silence. I needn't have worried. His high decibel snores shook the tree more than I did.

It was a long wait to the official breakfast. I strolled to the top of the gardens from where I could see the pepper pot lighthouse proudly sweeping the bay with its guiding light. I contemplated all that we had already experienced on just our first day. And how I was so determined to be the perfect pilgrim. And then it occurred to me that I had yet again broken another one of my pilgrim rules; there is no place for judgement on the Camino. Except I had. Judged. And not in a positive way. I didn't realise, until then, that I held "class-based" prejudices passed down from my father, who had been, at one time, president of the Queen's English Society. Need I say more? Those prejudices had the Brit, Andy sized up by his appearance and then by his London accent. My judgemental mind had heard exactly what its prejudice expected to. He had never said anything about big-arsed women walking the Camino. I had been completely mistaken. Well, I was obviously as full of shit as the next person. I wondered what other traits I would find out about myself along the way. In my very shaky defence, I would add that Andy told me at dinner that he, in turn, had thought I was "a snooty bird" as I walked around the albergue grounds with my hands clasped behind my back. He said I looked as though I was in the process of handing out rosettes at the Chelsea Flower Show. Not very flattering.

A tinge of pink started to mingle with the stars and finally I heard the albergue stirring into life. The long anticipated aroma of coffee reached me. What better way to start the day? A steaming mug of coffee was on its way. It had never tasted so good. Breakfast over, I went up to retrieve Boris and looked out the window. The Brit was hoiking his pack on his back. He had told us, last night, he was wild camping the Camino. I watched him stride out of the albergue grounds like a lone cowboy. I was surprised to feel disappointed to see him go. Without even a goodbye.

Chapter 5
STUFF THE SQUIRREL!

"A dragonfly arrives and leaves like a change of mind "

David Mitchell

Pedro and I sat in the early morning sun, lingering over our coffee, enjoying the beautiful surroundings of the Twelve Tribes albergue. Wanting to imprint it on our memories. But the Camino was calling us. We hit the trail, later than most pilgrims. Diola, the beautiful Nigerian woman, and Steffen, the young German, walked with us. We had only 6 kms to go before reaching San Sebastian, the jewel of the north coast, one of the most highly valued post codes in Spain.

Walking was delightful, along country lanes, with views opening over the bay of San Sebastian, shimmering in the morning sunlight. Donkeys thrust their heads over gates in greeting. They were my mum's favourite animal. I had frankly never seen the appeal before. Now I could so see why. I couldn't resist a moment with them. They contentedly accepted the ear scratching as their due. It must be a rite of pilgrim passage on the Camino del Norte. The donkeys sure didn't object to it. One last scratch as we walked away, and then their heads swivelled in unison toward the next batch of pilgrims.

We made our way on down into San Sebastián. Diola was leaving us here. She had friends from a previous French Camino in Pamplona to visit. I fussed over her, as was my tendency, even though she was a highly competent, independent woman. We had only just met but I already felt a deep sense of attachment to her. She tolerated my attentions with good grace. I made sure she had the exact directions to the bus station. And was clear on where she should go when she got to Pamplona. And that she had clean undies and a clean hankie. Well not quite, but not far off. We parted ways. I felt certain that it would not be for long. I made very sure to exchange numbers with her. She said she might catch up with us later. I was confident we would be seeing her again soon.

And then Pedro, Steffen, and I wound our way through the streets of San Sebastian, a place I knew really well from leading many a high school tour group around that beautiful city. Donostia, to give it its Basque name, is home to one of the most iconic beaches in Spain. A classic horseshoe shaped bay that snugly encircles the supremely golden sands of its main beach, La Concha. La Concha is a pristinely smooth sweep of yellow sand so perfect in proportion and colour, it looked like a postcard of itself. As if someone had been up all night meticulously colouring it in, just so, to conform with everyone's idea of classic seaside perfection. At the height of the summer, it was always crammed with bodies jostling for prime sunbathing position. And on this day it was just as crowded. Families were setting up basecamp with parasols, beach chairs and vast coolers of beer and sandwiches. Toddlers were building sandcastles; young lovers were rubbing suntan lotion into each other's shoulders. Walking past felt a little odd. Everyone was enjoying the early autumn sun, scantily clad, whilst we were armoured up in full walking gear.

Donostia also has a very well-deserved reputation as one of the premier foodie capitals of the world. It boasts many a Michelin starred restaurant. In the maze of streets that make up the old quarter every other doorway opens into a pintxos or tapas bar. True gourmets long to be invited into the inner circle of the famous gastronomic societies that were started up here in the mid 19th century. Fiercely private clubs as impenetrable as their Basque name, 'txokos'. Many of the unmarked and unremarkable doorways we walked past were portals into this hidden realm. They were originally male domains, and even today a few still are. Privy only to those fortunate enough to be born Basque and have a family member or be a close friend of someone in the know. Though even being born into the family of one of the clubs' presidents doesn't guarantee you access. There are long waiting lists. The tourist is firmly excluded, left only to salivate over what gastronomic delights those fortunate few get to savour. In my tour guide days, I would traipse the streets with my sweaty, often bored, flock trotting along behind me. My attention wasn't entirely focused on those alleyways and the hidden gateways to that foodie dimension. I was always looking up at the rolling hills above Mount Igueldo, the hill standing sentry at one end of the bay. I was longing to hike up there into the cool shady woods. I had no interest in the culinary clubs, I just wanted in on the secret beauty hidden up in those hills. Finally, I was about to get to fulfil that wish.

It was such a treat not to have 40 people in tow. Today I only had two and we were following the yellow arrows up into those hills. Over

Finding Love On The Camino

Monte Igueldo we went, leaving San Sebastian in our wake. We jostled for pole position between the three of us. They were faster on the uphills but I was nippy on the downhills. Often breaking into a trot. And it was just as enchanting as I had always imagined it to be. Conditions could not have been lovelier for walking. Gentle sunlight with little pillows of clouds in the pastel blue sky scudding along with us. Forest trails beckoned us into their tunnels of trees. They guided us along their paths lushly padded with ferns. Scented pine trees and ancient oaks either side of us. The air smelled so sweet it seemed it would be possible to break off a chunk of it, like chocolate, to taste it. We came out of these shaded trails blinking into the brightness of yet another sparkling seascape. It took our eyes a moment to adjust. Every pilgrim seemed to have the same visceral reaction on emerging out of the woods. Stopping to let their eyes adjust to the effect of all that light surrounding them on every side. Then staring, open mouthed, as if hypnotised by the sea view. The sun streaming down from above and being mirrored back by the sea. Sequins of sunlight chasing each other around the ocean surface in an endless game of tag.

The whole trail seemed deliberately planned to surprise and delight us at every turn. There was even a bit of old Roman road thrown into the mix. On we strode, tromping along pathways over which heavily armoured centurions had marched, before ceding their trails to pilgrims armed only with prayers and intentions. We passed rural communities, cow pastures, apple orchards and vineyards. I took it all in. I could enjoy it all. My mind was free from tour guide logistics. We stopped at a table laid with water and fruit for pilgrims. Someone had gone to all this trouble for our comfort and pleasure. I was humbled. This generosity made me more determined to be the best pilgrim I could be. On the table, too, was the all-important stamp for our pilgrim passports. Excellent. We could get our third official stamp. We pilgrims become quite obsessed with getting new stamps in our pilgrim passports. They can be stamped at albergues and bars along the way. Places often have their own personalised rubber stamps. They can be little works of art to remind us of a time and a place on our Camino. And then, when we finally reach Santiago, we show our passport at the pilgrim office if we wish to receive our Compostela, that official certificate proving we've walked the Camino.

We didn't linger long. We were soon back in action, picking up the pace as we moved along with the clouds. We overtook pilgrims as we went. My walking poles were making a hell of a racket on the tarmac as I clattered past. I'd lost my rubberised silencers. I issued a flurry of apologies for my clacking poles to every pilgrim we overtook. I assured them all that I would buy new rubber caps ASAP. I was trying to be the perfect pilgrim.

As I rounded the last corner on a downhill strait, I saw Sarah the Canadian from the previous night. Though she was ahead of me I knew it had to be her, a fit body in a grey walking skirt, moving at a very fast pace. I caught up with her and we exchanged pleasantries. I knew that Pedro and Steffen weren't far behind, and I didn't want them to catch up with me just yet. I was having too much fun walking on my own. She looked a tad surprised as I trotted away. A bit further on I found Richard with his bike waiting for her. Barely breaking my pace, I assured him Sarah wasn't far behind. Rounding the next bend, I paused to breathe in the scenery. Horses munching contentedly in the lush fields, the sea sparkling on my right. Just a quick breather though. I sensed, rather than saw, Pedro and Steffen hot on my heels. And I could see another hill just ahead.

We arrived just in time to snag ourselves bunks at the private albergue of San Martin in the village of Orio. It was 10 euros for a bed and dinner. Blimey, what a bargain. And I'd asked the all-important question. Yes, wine and beer were included. We were in. I sat outside to look out for Sarah and Richard. As they came past, I signalled them in. Now only a single bunk remained for one last lucky pilgrim. A familiar figure appeared over the brow of the hill. It was Andy, the lone cowboy. He said he was heading down to the river to camp and skin himself a squirrel for dinner. When he heard that a bed and a three-course meal, with beer, was on offer, all for the price of two pints back home, his sleeping bag was on that last bunk before you could say "wild camper."

I sat outside with Rosa, the hospitalera, the albergue was her labour of love. She was working tirelessly, calling her contacts, to find beds for the pilgrims she had had to turn away. She spoke only a few words of other languages besides Spanish. I happily acted as her translator for the non-Spanish speaking pilgrims. All the pilgrims finally had beds for the night. My Camino duty done. I did our washing. I hung our socks out on the washing line. They would enjoy a gorgeous view over the rolling hills as they dried in the late afternoon sun. Dinner would be in a little log cabin in the grounds at the usual time in Spain, 8pm.

Pedro, Steffen, Andy and I headed down the steep hill into the village. Andy was dressed in the most lurid green leggings. I was shocked. They were like something out of the movie 'Robin Hood Men in Tights'. Which is really the only place they should ever be seen. In the fishing village of Orio heads turned as he passed. Orio is on the river Oria that runs into the Bay of Biscay a kilometre or so away. I longed to dive into and explore the labyrinth of medieval alleyways in its old quarter. I could just make out buildings connected by tiny enclosed wooden bridges. The others weren't inclined to add further uphill kilometres to their day's tally. They wanted to sit and enjoy a beer. Just as Andy was about to snag the last table on the terrace of a bar on the main square, Pedro spotted the Choo Choo tourist train. Oh no. He couldn't be serious! This type of tourist train was the bane of our lives in Granada. It was always holding up the traffic! He held it, and all those who travelled on board, in great disdain. He would say that only tourists who were too lazy to walk used it. Surely, he didn't expect us to join the ranks of the lazy tourists.

He did! Once an idea took root within Pedro, there was no dissuading him. We reluctantly clambered aboard. We tried to mingle anonymously with the tourists in the crowded carriage. Andy's bright green tights made that impossible. The train deposited us at the waterfront. We found ourselves places at a bistro overlooking the Bay of Biscay. Music wafted from the bar as highly professional waiters swerved seamlessly around the tables attending to the tourists' needs. As well as a tourist destination, Orio was very much an alive and functioning fishing port. Our backdrop of multicoloured fishing trawlers and smaller boats were no mere adornments. We lingered over our drinks in the last rays of the day's sun.

Arriving anywhere late was never an option for me. Dinner back at the albergue was set to start at 8pm. I would not be late. Pedro refused to hurry. He had a more relaxed approach to timekeeping than even the Spanish! He was South American after all. One time, I got away with forwarding his watch half an hour until he cottoned on. For just a few happy days I no longer had to hassle him to hurry up for appointments. Oh well, it was good while it lasted. He was annoyed at my interfering. According to him, "I needed to let go." He said we lived in chilled southern Spain not stuffy old England. No-one cared if we arrived fifteen minutes late. No-one, that is, but me. I did care. To me it felt like a lack of respect to keep someone waiting. It didn't bother me to be kept waiting, but my palms would start sweating and I would become anxious when I thought someone was waiting for me. My fear of offending others by not doing the right thing was born of the more buttoned up, rule abiding culture of England. I couldn't bear to be judged as rude or ill mannered. Maybe no one did really mind if we didn't turn up on the dot for a meal that was seldom promptly served, and over which the whole point was to linger for hours shooting the breeze. But I couldn't bring myself to test out that theory. Particularly not as the perfect pilgrim.

Andy and I arrived back at the albergue breathless with seconds to spare while Pedro kept up his leisurely pace chatting with Steffen. We sat at the communal table. Sarah and Richard joined us. Pedro and Steffen ambled in. The meal was simple and delicious. The conversation was spirited. The wine flowed. Rosa sure knew what she was doing and did it tirelessly and with grace. She was one of the many Camino gems who run or volunteer to work in albergues, having themselves walked many a Camino. Pilgrims have their own tales of the impact these individuals have made on their experience. They offer kindness & empathy, as well as a bed for the night. She was full of motherly warmth handing out sage advice along with the dinner plates. She insisted on serving us herself and batted away all offers to help.

She had even carefully prepared a separate salad for me far from the glutinous breadcrumbs flying around the little kitchen. Her focus was firmly on the pilgrim and doing all she could to make their experience optimal.

We retired to our bunks full up with food, laughter and camaraderie. During the night I was awoken by the sound of the rain hammering down and the wind howling. I thought Andy must be glad not to be down by the river braving the elements with just a squirrel skin for added warmth. Snug and secure I smiled and drifted back to sleep.

Chapter 6
THE TILLEY HAT

If you think you're enlightened go spend a week with your family.

Ram Dass

T he storm howled through the night. By morning it had blown itself out leaving the day freshly laundered and sparkling with possibilities. In the log cabin of the Orio albergue, Pedro and I enjoyed our generous breakfast. At dinner with our fellow pilgrims, the night before, we had been effusive in our Camino camaraderie. We had said that today we would all walk together. But now, at breakfast, we were shy with them. We didn't want them to feel obliged to walk with us.

We set out at staggered times. No one wanting to cause embarrassment to the other. Except for Steffen, the gangly German youth. He seemed to have attached himself to Pedro and me. A sort of surrogate son. I wasn't entirely thrilled at the prospect. Steffen dawdled behind us. I think he sensed my reluctance to have him walk with us. Pedro and I discussed the situation and reckoned he would soon take off with people his own age. He was a nice enough kid. We were sure he would soon find his Camino tribe and be off partying, rather than trailing after a middle-aged couple like us. We slowed down a bit to let him catch up.

Then the three of us walked as we had the day before. We wove in and out of the other pilgrims on the trail at warp speed. Buen Camino-ing as we passed. And me continuing to apologise for my clacking walking poles. The morning flashed by us in a blur of hills, horses and harbours. We had a brief stop in Zarautz for coffee. I replenished my banana supply. And then the picture-perfect Basque villages came and went in a whirl. Their names emblazoned in the angular Basque lettering, bold faced and squat, mirroring the sharp sounds of the language. The spiky Basque flag proudly flying everywhere we flew.

Between Zarautz and Getaria we followed a narrow walkway between the highway and the sea. Jutting out in places over the ocean. I looked out over the edge and saw little fishing boats huddled in a corner of a tiny, improvised harbour between the pillars of the pathway and a wall, they nestled together like baby birds seeking comfort and warmth. We had protective barriers on both sides of us now, it felt like an extensive slalom run. Tunnels had been blasted out of the cliffs for the road at various stages. This major feat of engineering must have been quite some undertaking. I paused for a moment to watch a road crew at work hauling massive boulders into place behind wire meshing. The sheer amount of physical labour and bloody hard graft that went on behind the scenes to maintain the infrastructure of the Camino was quite awe inspiring.

And yet I couldn't help thinking that we pilgrims rock along taking it all for granted. So bound up are we in our own journeys we are barely aware that each village we pass through has a tireless force of Camino volunteers making our lives easier. Painting the yellow arrows, clearing the paths, slogging tirelessly in the albergues. They lay out offerings of water, snacks and the all-important stamps for our pilgrim passports. As I took the slalom bends, I wondered if we were an inconvenience to the locals. I suppose it was inevitable that we were. Given that we were only ever passing through these places, barely skimming the surface of their lives we were never made aware of it. Part of me would have loved to have sat down in each village and ask the locals questions. I hankered to know what it was like to be in and of these communities. And how they perceived us, the pilgrims. They gave us so much, all we left in our wake was a few euros in tips and our heartfelt thanks and appreciation. I hoped it was enough.

Down to sea level again we trogged across beaches not letting the heaviness of our sand incrusted shoes slow our pace. We entered the village of Zumaia, along its plane tree lined walkway. The tops of the trees reaching out and clasping one another overhead. We sat to catch our breath and contemplated the contrast between the industrialised port and the old town. While we were sitting there a Tilley hatted pilgrim came toward us. A Tilley hat is a Canadian invention, a floppy hat made to last forever. Our Canadian Gucci Camino clients always wore a Tilley hat. Practical they undoubtedly are. The height of sartorial elegance they definitely are not. They are the sort of practical acquisition that seems like a good idea at the time. There is a place inside the brim of each hat to put your home address in case it should ever stray from your head. I always imagined the holiday maker's dismay at having 'mislaid' their hat, only to have it triumphantly turn up at their home address shorty after their return from holiday.

Finding Love On The Camino

It was strange that this Tilley hatted pilgrim didn't have his Canadian flag emblazoned in full view on his pack. Most Canadians do. As the Tilley hat bobbed closer to us, I got ready to issue a 'Buen Camino'. The hat wearer was firmly focused on his feet, head down. As he drew alongside us the 'Buen Camino' died on my lips, and it turned into a surprised 'Andy!' It was Andy! How was this possible? He had left the Orio albergue way ahead of us. Even travelling at our brisk pace, it was unlikely that our paths would cross. We stared at him in amazement. This was a serendipitous meeting. We decided to go and get a coffee and plan the rest of the day together.

Finding a cafe wasn't easy, most places were setting up for lunch. The waiters were smoothing white tablecloths and laying down place settings. We considered just pressing on to the next town, but the idea of coffee had taken root. We rounded a corner in a much less touristy backstreet. There we found an ordinary neighbourhood bar. No waiters and white tablecloths here. The tables were covered with chequered oilskin and the locals were leisurely sipping their coffee. There was a free table on the terrace and so we happily dropped our backpacks. It felt good to slow down for a bit, take the weight off, sit and enjoy the moment instead of charging on ahead.

I was about to enter the cafe to order our coffee when a non-local emerged out of the door. It was Richard! I couldn't believe it. And inside was Sarah! We all hugged each other. All our breakfast shyness was gone. Over steaming hot cups of coffee, we revelled in the same easy camaraderie of the previous evening. We had reconnected so effortlessly. The Camino had placed us all in each other's way. It was Sarah's birthday. To celebrate she and Richard had booked private accommodation in Zumaia. We didn't want to impose ourselves on them. We said we would join them just for coffee, and then leave them to enjoy their private celebration. But Sarah insisted that we meet up with them for lunch. There was an albergue nearby. It had formally been a convent for cloistered nuns, El Convento de San Jose. So, we decided to try our luck there.

We joined the short line by the convent side door. Pedro and I were allocated a nun's cell. It was stark and a little damp. A huge crucifix loomed over the twin beds to dissuade us from any ideas of hanky panky. As I pulled my sleeping bag out of Boris and laid it on my single bed, I realised that I would have been happy to have swapped the privilege of our private cell for the fun and laughter of the communal dorm. I was sure Pedro felt the same way. We prepared our bunks in silence. After 19 years together we were comfortable in our companionship. The initial fireworks of our romance had burnt down to a damp squib that would take a lot to reignite. But then that happens to every couple, doesn't it? Our relationship wasn't perfect but whose was? I banished these thoughts from my mind. This wasn't the time for introspection. Here, on the Camino, life was uncomplicated, and very much in the now. And right now, we were both way too hungry to consider an amorous approach, even if one had been forthcoming.

Andy and Steffen were hungry too. Sarah and Richard had invited us to lunch so we joined them at the restaurant they had chosen. We ordered the pilgrim meal. Many restaurants, along the Camino offer a pilgrim menu. For a modest price you get a three-course meal including wine. Pilgrim perks! As if being a pilgrim wasn't already wonderful enough. We toasted Sarah's special day. My tour guide instinct kicked in. There can be no birthday celebration without a birthday cake. I excused myself from the table to find the best cake shop in town. I returned with cake and candles and sneaked them past Sarah. The restaurant was happy to oblige. More wine was quaffed. Laughter rolled around the table. Then it was time for birthday cake. The cake was carried from the kitchen by a waiter singing *"Que los cumplas feliz"*, "Happy birthday to you". The other tables joined in the chorus, as they do in Spain, revelling in this excuse for a joyful celebration. Sarah's beaming face was a picture as she blew out the candles. A picture that I snapped for posterity. A treasured memory of the simple joy of this Camino moment, camaraderie, laughter and fun.

Lunch and birthday cake over we all agreed it was time to order dinner. I took charge. I conferred with Pedro. We ordered a selection of 'pintxos', the Basque version of tapas. A procession of local fare emerged from the kitchen; boquerones - sardines in olive oil, calamares, prawns, tortilla, red piquillo peppers, goat's cheese. The flavours were enhanced by generous amounts of garlic and paprika. We were all stuffed just like the pimientos peppers they served. Dinner over it was that special time, post dinner drinks. With what should we make the final birthday toast? The inspired answer came to me. Pacharan. Pacharan is a local digestif from the neighbouring state of Navarra. It is made from sloe berries steeped in an aniseed-based liquor. The most common brand is 'Zoco'. I love 'Zoco'. It comes in a satisfyingly hefty glass bottle, so you don't knock it over when you've had a few. After we'd been Zoco'd we lost track of the time. Shit. We had forgotten the curfew. We had seven minutes to leg it back up the steep hill to the convent. We left Sarah and Richard to the rest of their evening. Convent curfews were not to be messed with. Even Pedro had to hustle.

Earlier, before our final toast to Sarah, and while we could still remember our mobile numbers, we created a Camino WhatsApp group. Now we were connected. All shyness between us was gone. We could check in with one another anytime we wanted. As we sprinted up the hill to the convent albergue I realised, with delight, that I may have just become part of a Camino family!

Chapter 7

NO ROOM AT THE INN

If you can't fly then run, if you can't run then walk, if you can't walk then crawl,

but whatever you do you have to keep moving forward."

Martin Luther King Jr

N o breakfast was served at the convent albergue. No bar next door. No pre-walk coffee close by. Pedro and Steffen decided we should start walking and then find coffee along the way. I was still trying to compute this when Andy turned up. I filled him in. He was not convinced either. Oh well, I guessed all I had to do was to put one foot in front of the other and find out if this was possible.

Andy and I trailed behind Pedro and Steffen with just the one thing on our minds. Morning coffee. Dawn was breaking. I could hear angels singing. Was the lack of caffeine affecting my senses? I glanced over at Andy to see if he was hearing it too. He didn't appear to be. The voices were getting louder. I had heard of Camino miracles happening. Was this one? As we rounded the next bend a little chapel was ahead of us. That was where the song was coming from. The inhabitants of this tiny hamlet were inside singing as the sun rose on a glorious morning on the Camino. I could tell that even the squirrel skinning Andy was affected by it all.

Steffen and Pedro kept up their long-legged pace ahead of us. Andy and I fell naturally into a short-legged stride. We were totally at ease in each other's company. No worries about possible misinterpretations of the other's intentions. He surprised me. He had an original take on things. One minute we were talking about very ordinary matters and the next we were having the wildest philosophical and metaphysical discussions. Including off planet and everywhere in between. Amazingly, ten undulating kilometres sped past before we found breakfast. Finally, coffee! With delicious thick egg and potato omelette that the Spanish call tortilla. And cider. Alcoholic, of course. Naturally it would have been rude to refuse. I sat back replete. There is nothing like that Camino sensation of pure joy in the moment.

Now, post coffee, we could really get moving. We walked a mix of roads, forest trails and country paths. At one point we crossed over a motorway, and I experienced an abrupt and jarring incursion of the non-walking world. I looked down at the traffic whooshing by underfoot and felt I could catch a glimpse of myself, nose pressed to the window of that Gucci Camino touring bus, looking up longingly at these hills sweeping past in a blur. And here I was walking in those same hills. It seemed nuts that we would ever choose to blast through all this beauty in a bus or even a car. The rolling hills and the patchwork of lush pastures was like walking over the surface of a giant chocolate box, straight out of an advert for Swiss chocolate. And then, as if that wasn't enough, we would round another corner and be greeted by yet another beautiful sea view as the early autumn sun bounced around the waves in the Bay of Biscay. When I had my nosed pressed up against that tour bus window, I could never have imagined that it would be quite this beautiful.

The yellow arrows were now leading us away from the coast. We were making our way further up into the hills. No more sea views until we reached Bilbao in a few days' time. It was onwards and lots of upwards. Yes, the relentless up and downhill of the Basque Country was every bit as real as we had heard. We followed the well-marked trail past vertiginously sloping pastures on which the sheep, horses and cows somehow remained improbably vertical, as if velcroed on. They were like the animals on the 'fuzzy felt' boards of my childhood, where the felt animals clung like magic to the flocked backing board.

We slogged our way up one more sheer slope and stopped a while at the top, panting heavily and looking back, congratulating ourselves for making it over the almost vertical incline. Behind us blasted a wiry, athletic local barely breaking a sweat. We watched, bent over our walking poles, bodies heaving with the exertion as he pounded effortlessly past us. We had barely enough breath to greet him as he swept by us on his way. It appeared the locals too wore fuzzy felt on the soles of their running shoes. I was sorely tempted to lift up his feet to check. But I would have had to catch him first and that wasn't going to happen.

The surfeit of sheer stunning beauty took my attention away from my aching muscles. We were immersed in a 360-degree panoramic view of perfectly formed mountain ranges and lush animal strewn pastures.

Huge, powerful horses munched their way across precipitous slopes. Some had massive cowbells, somewhat ignominiously I felt, slung around their muscular necks. They showed not the slightest interest in us. The donkeys were another matter, with their appealing sad doe eyes and fluffy heads, they were always up for a quick chat and a cuddle. And we passed a goat, with long shaggy hair, a beard and the most impressive horns. He, and his kind, must have been the inspiration for Billy Goat Gruff. He was no doubt confused by the constant barrage of photos we were taking of him. "Who is this Billy Goat Gruff of whom you all speak?" He could have made a killing if he'd charged by the photo. Further on, scarecrows guarded the cornfields and the vineyards. Some wore shirts emblazoned with Basque slogans, the only part of which I could make out was the emphatic punctuation. Exclamation marks abounded. Were they warning us of something? Maybe we would be shot if we nicked a grape, maybe wishing us Buen Camino, maybe protesting over some local dispute, who knew?!!! I sure didn't. But I sure wanted to.

As Pedro and Steffen disappeared over the next rise, Andy and I clocked a lone figure trudging along ahead of us. "Buen Camino" I called out to her as we nipped on past. "How's it going?" She answered, "Not so good". I called out some empty words of encouragement and we left her behind us. Andy and I walked on in silence. I was ashamed for not stopping to find out why she was "not so good". A+pilgrims don't behave this way. But we were so close to our destination, and I just wanted to get the relentless hills behind me. We kept walking in silence. Until we couldn't. We both knew what had to be done. And without saying anything we turned and headed back to her.

Her name was Celine. She didn't seem surprised that we had come back for her. She was defeatedly exhausted. She handed Andy her backpack before he had even finished offering to carry it for her. It was a very heavy old-fashioned contraption and must have been horribly uncomfortable for her to carry. She was French, she told us. She had walked from her hometown of La Rochelle. Bloody hell! That meant she had already covered about 450 kms. She was beautiful in that dishevelled, effortless Gallic way. Delivered of her backpack, she went off to relieve herself behind a tree. I nudged Andy and remarked on how attractive she was. I knew he was single. "Imagine falling in love on the Camino!" I said, "How romantic would that be?"

After half an hour the extremely welcome sight of Markina came into view. Pedro and Steffen waved us in from the packed terrace of the bar in the town square. Boris slid off me with a sigh. I went in to order wine and beers at the bar. And a glass of milk for Steffen. I had to repeat my request for milk a number of times, it's not a done thing in Spain. Is it a done thing anywhere else?

It was time to claim our beds at the municipal albergue. Pedro came with me. We didn't get further than the front door. There was a handwritten sign saying "Completo" or "Full". Oh well. A private albergue it would have to be then. Except that the private albergues were "Completo" as well. Now I understood why Sarah and Richard had recommended we pre-book in this town. They had snagged themselves a private room.

When we returned to the bar, a woman at the next table was explaining something in broken English to the others. She was saying that the town was full due to a local festival. She kindly offered to take us, in her truck, to the albergue of Zenarruza 7 kms down the road. But I knew only four would fit in her truck at a squeeze, not five. I was not going to abandon the French pilgrim, Celine. I immediately offered to hoof it to the Zenarruza albergue. That way Celine could ride in the truck with the others. Steffen, still fresh as a daisy, offered to run with me.

I felt a second wind at the prospect of a pre-dinner run unencumbered by Boris, my backpack. It would be fun. The others raised no objections, they were bushed. I set off at a trot Steffen loped on ahead. Bless his cotton socks. He pretended to be taking pictures, waiting for me to catch up with him. I told him to go ahead so he'd have time to shower, it was already nearly dinner time. But he gallantly stopped and waited for me. He could have covered the distance in half the time. It did occur to me that my husband hadn't been so gallant. But then I had offered to do this.

Finally, we arrived at the medieval monastery at Zenarruza. Me sweaty and panting, Steffen still with a marathon in him. I barely registered the beauty of the setting as we had only minutes to spare before dinner. Pedro was hanging up his socks in the drying room next to the shower. I hastily got undressed. I left my walking clothes in a heap outside the door. I thought Pedro might grab them and wash them for me. When I emerged from the shower they were still sitting in a heap where I'd left them. No time now. I would do them after dinner.

I threw on my one change of clothes and legged it upstairs for dinner. Huge hunks of bread were being devoured. The main and only course was a pasta-based minestrone soup served with the beer produced in the monastery. That was gluten with a side serving of gluten washed down by gluten. Not good. That would put a celiac like me out of action for days. Pedro was devouring his. Andy asked the monk, at the head of the table, if I might have some salad or tortilla? The monk didn't deign to answer, just looked scornful. Well, this was a by donation albergue, what they call a donativo on the Camino. I could hardly expect to order a la carte. I had covered at least 42 kms that day. I would have to add a few more to my tally.

There was a bar just a kilometre down the road. Before I left, I asked Pedro if he wouldn't mind rinsing out my walking gear for me. Off I trotted again this time under the night sky. The squat rustic bar appeared like a mirage. Smoke belching from its chimney. I waded through ankle deep paper napkins to get to the bar. The custom of dropping your used napkin to the floor had still not died out in this remote village. The napkins got swept up at the end of the night.

There was a welcoming wave of heat from the roaring fire. But that was all that welcomed me, no friendly barman. Tables had been stripped of their paper cloths. The place had that used up, wrung out feel of a very long and very boozy lunch party. Sort of like me. Minus the booze and the party. I called out an "hola" in the direction of the kitchen. Eventually a weary barman appeared. He said I was welcome to have drinks but no food. The kitchen was closed.

My eyes fell upon a huge hunk of tortilla sweating under a plastic dome. The waiter followed my ravenous gaze. He served me up the whole massive wedge. It was the size of a paving slab. He offered to heat it up for me, but I had it out of his hands before he could finish the sentence. I ordered a glass of local txakoli white wine and settled in by the fire to scarf it down. Never had tortilla tasted so good. And I've eaten a lot of tortilla. With the paving slab in my belly and warmed by the fire and the txakoli I would have dropped off to sleep right there. But the door opened. Pedro, Steffen, Celine and Andy walked in.

They had discovered that there was no curfew at the albergue. Pedro was delighted. I'd like to think that he'd come down to keep me company. Maybe he had. But I fear it was the chance of a few late-night drinks that spurred him to walk the extra kilometre. No matter. It was lovely to gather at the day's end like this. Swap stories and laughter. We toasted the day, and of course, finished with that potent brew of sloe berries steeped in aniseed liquor, Pacharan.

When I arrived back at the albergue my sweaty heap of clothes was still sitting where I'd left it.

Chapter 8

TXIRIMIRI

Souls tend to go back to who feels like home.

N.R. Hart

As my companions got ready to tuck themselves into their bunk beds, I dashed down to the bathrooms to rinse out my stinky clothes. I had my fingers and toes crossed that my hiking gear would be dry by the time we left in the morning. I was exhausted. And I was anxious. In my rush to get to dinner I had committed that most unpardonable of sins. I hadn't organised my backpack. I didn't want to wake everyone up with my zipping and unzipping and rustling and scrunching as I searched Boris for my toothbrush. On the scale of pilgrim misdemeanours, I knew this would score me a definite pilgrim D grade.

I tiptoed back into the dorm. As I got to my bunk, muted mutterings were coming from the middle of the room. In the dark I searched my backpack for my toothbrush. In front of me a most interesting drama was unfolding. I realised, with relief, that no one was going to notice the noise I was making. So, I got to and reorganised Boris from my front row seat.

What was taking place was possibly the closing act of a drama that I had been unknowingly witnessing over the last few days. Along the trail we would occasionally bump into a handsome young Italian chap who was walking with two extremely beautiful women. His name was Mario. The younger woman was Klara, she was German, and the older woman was Spanish, Miriam. They all seemed to me to be having a jolly old time together, laughing and singing. The women would sit either side of Mario at our communal dinners. They would walk with him arm in arm, as a threesome, along the trail.

But over the last few days I'd seen the dynamic between them change. A definite element of competition had entered the scene. The two women were vying for Mario's attentions and his affections. They were competing with one another for the prize, and he was the prize. They raced each other to be the one to buy him a coffee. There was even a physical skirmish in a bar to get the seat next to him. Mario appeared blithely oblivious to it all. I pointed it out to Pedro. We had our money on the Spaniard, Miriam. She exuded a toughness lacking in the younger, Klara.

The ruckus in the centre of the dorm was coming from Miriam. She was playing a blinder. She was the last lone pilgrim to have been admitted into the albergue. She was standing in the middle of the dorm with her backpack, with nowhere to sleep. Every single bunk was already occupied. The hospitalero was called for. He stood alongside her scratching his head at the dilemma. Obviously, someone had messed up the bed count and it was far too late to send Miriam out into the night to walk on to the next albergue.

I saw the gleam in the Spanish woman's eye. She saw her opportunity and jumped all over it. "It's OK," she cooed. "I'll share with Mario!" She selflessly offered. The hospitalero was profuse in his thanks. What a generous act. No pilgrim D grade for Miriam. She got the approval of everyone. Well almost everyone. I looked over at Klara. Her shoulders had slumped in defeat. She'd been trumped and she knew it. Miriam triumphantly grabbed her sleeping bag and leapt on to Mario's bunk. The next day I saw Klara walking on alone.

I contemplated love on the Camino as I fell asleep. Couples certainly did form here. Were Mario and Miriam to become another Camino love story? Would they walk off into a Camino sunset and raise little bilingual Italo-Hispanic pilgrims? Or would Klara up her game? I was just happy that I was all set with my husband, thank you. I'd left those shenanigans far behind me in my past. Though it did surprise me to realise that it hadn't occurred to me to offer Miriam my bunk. I could have snuggled down alongside Pedro.

+++++++++

I woke up to another glorious Camino sunrise. The smell of baking bread wafted through the dorm and then came the smell I love. Coffee. There was coffee. That was all that mattered. Today we all walked together, as a group, Pedro, me, Andy, Steffen and our new friend the beautiful Celine. We switched easily in and out of each other's company. We were all firmly focused on our goal for the day, the town of Gernika, 25kms away.

Finding Love On The Camino

We strode along more forest trails. We passed miniature toy-town chapels. We walked through more villages of A-framed Basque houses, with their balconies filled with flowers. I romped along in my Camino bubble of sunshine. Everything was lit up with glorious golden light. And then, the theme of the day changed. It became babbling brooks and bridges. Some of those bridges were made of wood, some were mere steppingstones, and some were made of solid stone dating back centuries. It was impossible not to imagine the thousands of pilgrims who had walked over them.

Celine and I chatted as we walked. My French soon became well oiled. She was naturally beautiful, with a certain resilience or maybe toughness about her. She told me how she was walking the Camino to find a new sense of purpose, a new direction in her life. She had left a failed business back in France and, as well, she was giving herself time to contemplate and resolve a complicated relationship she was in. She said she was low on funds, but the Camino always provided. She had walked all the way from her hometown of La Rochelle. She told me how she walked 230 kms to Bordeaux before she connected with the French Camino, the Chemin Le Puy. She told me that when she could walk no further, she slept in town parks and playgrounds. Sometimes, as nightfall approached, she would knock on the front door of a house and introduce herself as a pilgrim and ask for a meal and a bed for the night. She said this with such a natural air, as if anyone would do the same in her position. Blimey. I could never do that. I imagined the furtive whispered conversations in the kitchen; "What do you mean you don't know her either?!" "I thought she was a friend of yours!" "No, I thought that you knew her!" Too late, they couldn't turn her away. Man, she had balls. I knew I could learn a thing or two from her.

We walked into Gernika. It felt more than a little surreal. A place so intrinsically linked with repression and terror. Until then the town had really only existed in my mind as Picasso's stark, enormous mural on the walls of the Reina Sofia Art Museum in Madrid. The mural represented the moment this little Basque town had been relentlessly strafed by Hitler's Luftwaffe during the Spanish Civil War. Franco let them use Gernika as a testing ground for their firepower. I had given many a talk to mainly disinterested US teenagers, humouring me with their feigned attention, on the enormity and importance of this iconic representation of the horrors of war. It felt not only surreal but disrespectful to go yomping through this place in such a joyous frame of mind. However, the feel of the place was not one of repressed pain and suffering but quite the opposite; that of a light, optimistic, forward-thinking community.

We met Sarah and Richard at a private albergue they had forward scouted for us. The first thing I saw when we got there was the unmistakable tall, erect figure of Diola. She came forward with her graceful, measured pace to greet us. I bounded up to her like a Labrador puppy, effusive in my greeting, wagging my tail. I was delighted to see her. She, in turn, was happy to see us in her calmer, considered way. And so, with Pedro, myself, Sarah and Richard, Andy, Steffen and Celine, we were all together at the albergue. Hooray!

We headed out to lunch to celebrate our reunion. When we were checking in to the albergue we met a delightful young English woman called Kaitlin. She had just graduated university and was walking the

Camino on her own. I invited her to join us for lunch. Pedro had found us a great restaurant, slightly swankier than usual. We sat on its terrace in the sun. Pedro struck up a conversation with the restaurant owner, as was his tendency. He has an amazing ability to form instant bonds with people. I hoped the poor chap didn't feel overwhelmed by Pedro's attentions.

We ordered a selection of pintxos and raciones, dishes to share, on the recommendation of the owner. We had Bacalao Biskaina, salted cod floating in a heavenly pepper, onion and garlic sauce. Beans baked in tomatoes and garlic, so delicious that I would never again be able to eat the tinned English equivalent without weeping at the comparison. Gorgeous grilled peppers and seared tuna that was so soft it flaked deliciously off my fork. And to finish our meal, the local idiazabal cheese with quince jelly and raisins. All accompanied by the local txakoli white wine. Bliss. This was no pilgrim's menu. This was a celebration.

I chatted with Kaitlin. She was walking the Camino the whole way by herself. She was walking to decide what she wanted to do next. She had a vague idea of doing some volunteering work on community ecological projects in southern Spain. She said that she relished the time and space alone in which to mull over her decisions. I tried to imagine doing the Camino by myself. Diola joined in our conversation. She said that she too was perfectly happy walking alone. She said the trick was to avoid the bickering middle aged couples. Really? "They are not a barrel of laughs," she said. I was sure there must be more to it than that. I admired both women so much. It felt to me an extremely brave thing to do to choose to walk the Camino alone. To find your own company enough. To have the self-confidence to introduce yourself and spend time with fellow pilgrims, then to choose to leave them and move on by yourself. Particularly at Kaitlin's young age. She was actively choosing her own company over that of others. She was entirely comfortable in her own skin. She inspired me. Not that I had the least intention of walking the Camino on my own.

Kaitlin asked about our future plans and when we would be heading back to the UK. I was confused. Why on earth would I be heading to England? Slowly it dawned on me that she had assumed that Andy and I were a couple! What on earth could have given her that impression. I was taken aback. Surely it was obvious to all that I was with the tall, handsome Argentinian chap? I looked at it from her point of view. Pedro was on the other side of the table from us. He had invited the restaurant owner to come and sit next to him. They were deep in conversation, in Spanish, exchanging numbers, talking of a possible future collaboration where we bring our own pilgrim groups through here in the future. I felt Pedro was getting a little ahead of himself. We had spoken of starting our own hiking tours, but in Andalucia. The Basque Country was a long way from southern Spain. But certainly, there was nothing to suggest to Kaitlin that we were more than fellow pilgrims. There was no handholding or loving glances. But then again there was most certainly nothing to suggest that Andy and I were more to each other than that either!

The next day we had our first day of rain. This was definitely not txirimiri (pronounced 'chirimiri'). Txirimiri is a particularly lovely, and for once pronounceable, Basque word. And it's my favourite and only Basque word. It means a light drizzle. But this wasn't a light drizzle.

Finding Love On The Camino

This was the sort of rain that somehow defies the laws of gravity and comes at you from all directions. It swirls at you from behind, from in front, from the sides and even up at you from the trail. We were hoping to make Bilbao today, 32 kms away.

We started with a long, steep uphill climb. It was treacherous, cloying mud and slippery stones. We strung out along the trail. We being Pedro, myself, Steffen, Andy, Sarah and Richard, Diola and Celine. Not so much chatting today. We were all locked in our own private battle with the rain, the hills and the mud. I tried invoking the Camino spirit to counteract the relentlessness of the rain's grip on both my soggy body and my soggy mind. But once you let those damp thoughts seep in through the seams, they're in for the duration.

The mud seemed to have become a living entity with a voracious appetite for our shoes. You tentatively raised your foot to feel its mouth sucking insatiably at your footwear, desperate to devour it. Barefoot probably wouldn't have been a bad option. The trail was now like a ski run made of sludge. We were sliding, but with walking, rather than ski, poles. It was hard enough for me to keep my balance, even with the aid of my sticks. Those walking without them were having a right old time of it. But there was nothing that I could do to help them. They could only adopt a tentative, mincing step, their arms held wide in airplane fashion as they teetered their way gingerly along. On the downhill black graded runs some just gave in and slid down on their bums. We were all so heavily plastered in mud anyway it didn't make that much difference.

I kept looking out to my right as we rounded each bend, searching for the sea. I love the ocean. Both its shimmering surface and all the majesty that lies beneath it. For almost 10 years I had lived out my Jacques Cousteau fantasy. Filming dolphins, eagle rays and sharks in the beautiful Caribbean Sea. I now yearned for its companionship. Today was hard going.

Diola, despite her long legs, fell behind us. I wondered if she was regretting catching up with us only to be left to walk alone. I hoped she would be OK. The village of Lezama was the last resting place before the final stretch into Bilbao. It came and went without any of us connecting. I put my head down and focused on the goal of Bilbao. Bilbao was a city that Pedro and I loved. Only 11 kms to go. To keep my mind off the mud I reminisced about Bilbao in the old days, the early 90's when I had first started taking groups of US high school students there. Back then it had been a grim and grimy city.

On the outskirts of Bilbao, someone with a particularly sadistic sense of humour had been out moving the signposts around. I'd passed a sign saying that the centre of Bilbao was 8 kms away. I was sure I was closer than that. And then I went another kilometre only to pass another sign that said the centre of Bilbao was 8 kms away. My energy levels were dipping. When this sort of thing happened, I could usually remind myself of the great joy and privilege of being on the Camino, doing what I loved best, and I could feel the resulting surge in energy propelling me on. Not today. The best I could manage was to remind myself that no one was holding a gun to my head. No one was forcing me to walk anywhere. Hell, I could jump in that passing taxi if I chose to. I would have to clean some mud off myself first, but it was always an option for me. All I was asking of myself was to put one muddy foot in front of the other.

Finding Love On The Camino

Rounding a corner a yellow arrow smirked at me, I swear it winked, as it pointed me up a long, steep path. Well, not so much a path as a vertical mud bog. If this turned out to be one of those deviations that takes you up a track only ever meant for a particularly sure-footed goat, just to marvel at a tiny chapel identical to the last fifteen you had seen, I was not going to be amused. Moreover, those chapels were always closed so you could not even shelter in them from the rain. But I obediently followed the arrows up into that vertical bog. More arrows ahead confirmed that this was the right path. I sludged on, head down.

Pedro caught up with me as I was dragging my sorry, soggy, muddy bottom through the streets of Bilbao willing the albergue to miraculously appear. In front of us was a local feria. The only English equivalent I can think of is a street party. But the two occasions couldn't be more different. A local feria anywhere in Spain has its own unique flavour revolving around spontaneity, fun and love of life fuelled by copious amounts of food and wine. Quite different from the tea drinking, stiff upper lipped, slightly self-conscious flag waving British version. The flavour of this feria was pulpo or octopus. The smell and warmth emanating from large copper pots was definitely enticing. I was reticent about barging in uninvited to this very local affair. Pedro wasn't concerned. He struck up a conversation with some of the men who graciously welcomed us in. I felt uncomfortable gate crashing like this, but I knew Pedro loved this stuff and I didn't want to deprive him of the experience. Everyone was generous and warm towards us. I couldn't imagine a couple of grubby, soggy Basques turning up unannounced to a British street party and being treated with this generosity of spirit.

We finally made it to the Albergue Santa Cruz de Begoña, a small albergue, the first to appear on the trail, I had feared it might be full but fortunately there was plenty of room. Probably because it hadn't been made to sound too appealing in the Camino guides. It had been described as very basic with just the one shower for all, and from the outside it didn't look too welcoming. Small and squat. It was wedged between high rise flats. A little shabby and forlorn looking. But the reception from the hospitalera soon dispelled any doubts, her smile eclipsed them all. She surged forward with a burst of energy and warmth to receive us, relieving us immediately of our packs which surely weighed more than her. She heaved them effortlessly up, and ushered us in. We removed our muddy shoes at the entrance, but our clothing was still caked in mud, and we were dripping all over the floor. She batted away our apologies and settled us in, wielding a mop in our wake. With her no nonsense, kind and compassionate welcome the warmth she exuded raised our spirits and made us forget the trials and tribulations of the mud-fest we had just endured. One by one our friends filed in, sodden and a little dejected. All were immediately boosted by her spirit and relaxed into the warmth of her welcome. Her name was Kati. She was a tiny, coiled spring of effervescent energy and goodness. She even gave us our own private dorm room. We set about preparing for our communal dinner. I could sense her observing us. She commented on how much fun we were having. And then I will never forget what she said next. She said, "Camino families that come together at the start of the Camino never finish the Camino together."

Santiago de Compostela, the official end of the Camino, was 650 kms away. What constellation would we form as we walked into the cathedral square? I mused. Would it just be Pedro and me? I could see how that could be the case. It made me sad to think that. The next morning, I woke up and saw, as Kati had described them, my Camino family surrounding me. I loved that. And the rain had stopped, not even a hint of txirimiri.

Chapter 9

TENT CITY

"You can't save a person who doesn't want to be saved."

Pearl Cleage

Bilbao sparkled. The streets were washed clean, inviting us to linger a while. Sarah and Richard were keen to get out and see the sights. And so, Pedro and I slipped easily into our role as tour guides.

Taking groups around Spain in the very early 90's I used to feel the need to talk up this rather unprepossessing city. In those days Bilbao was only just starting the process of renovation, morphing itself from an ugly duckling into a swan. Back then, it had felt grubby and grimy and frankly a little depressing. Heavy on industry, light on beauty. Not so now. The Basque people are quite rightly enormously proud of Bilbao. Where so many other cities have failed to truly reinvent themselves, resulting in a Europe wide homogeneous experience of bland shopping-malled city centres, Bilbao has succeeded triumphantly.

The city has become the role model for reinvention, whilst protecting and nurturing all that is so unique about Basque-ness in a dignified manner. It is truly a city where culture abounds. Bilbao does not need to flaunt its uniqueness; it simply is so. Difficult to define, it has a hum and a spark all of its own. It never fails to surprise and delight me.

Walkways have been unobtrusively developed alongside the river making it the perfect place to stroll, jog and skate. There is a funicular ride that takes you up into the hills for wonderful views out over the city, the surrounding mountains and beyond to the sea. La Ribera, the covered market, is still a real and thriving hub for locals to do their daily shopping. And Plaza Nueva is my very favourite main square in Spain. I love to sit there, and people watch. Bilboa's flagship is, of course, the Guggenheim art museum which attracts many thousands of visitors every year. But the city is so much more than that. It is quirky and fascinating, and Pedro and I spent a happy day showing Sarah and Richard around all the nooks and crannies of this beautiful city. We ended the day with a dilemma.

We were to meet Diola, Celine, Andy and Steffen at an albergue just a short 15 kms away in Barrakaldo. Sarah, Richard, Pedro and I had already spent the day walking more miles than we had intended to around the city. And according to all the guide books, the walk out of Bilbao to Barrakaldo is dire, kilometres of grim industrialised landscape. What to do? The decision was unanimous. We took the metro to Barrakaldo. Despite all my best intentions to be a perfect pilgrim this was a major transgression. Tomorrow I would have to do better.

In Barrakaldo we pretty much had the albergue to ourselves. The hospitalera, Norma, was Argentinian. I was so happy for Pedro. He had a compatriot, from his beloved Argentina, with whom to reminisce and share a 'maté', (a beverage made from a blend of herbs from the Argentinian Sierra). He missed his homeland dreadfully. We, of course, invited Norma to join us for dinner. She was one of the many hospitaleros who volunteer to work in albergues all of whom have some deep connection with the Camino, usually having walked their own and having been forever transformed, wishing to pay forward a little of what the Camino has given to them. She seemed to be a slightly troubled but very well-meaning soul.

It had quickly become our custom to end our evening meals with the fiery digestif Pacharan. And since the evening of Sarah's birthday, Zoco had been our favourite brand. That heavy bottle, that would never get accidentally knocked over, was way too heavy to carry with us in our backpacks. We had to finish it off. We might have taken Norma a Pacharan too far. She assured us that she would be up early to unlock the albergue doors the next morning. However, as I stumbled blearily from my bunk, I came across the statuesque figure of Diola. She was backpacked, walking poles in hand staring at the door willing it to let her be on her way. I was surprised it didn't. Diola was one of those people who naturally commanded attention. She possessed formidable inner strength and persuasive powers. Had I been a door I would definitely have succumbed to her will.

Finding Love On The Camino

Eventually we were all back on the road leaving the metropolis of Bilbao behind. Chimneys, turbines, and the industrial landscape receded behind us as highways became roads, roads became paved paths, paths became sandy trails. Today we would be saying goodbye to the Basque Country. We were heading to the town of Castro Urdiales, in the next province along, Cantabria. The sunshine held out long enough to illuminate the glorious coastline. Underfoot it was slippery. There had been rain throughout the night. We traversed a steady series of coastal hills, paying careful attention to our step on the way down. I was delighted to meet up again with my friend, the Atlantic Ocean. I knew this cold corner of the coastline was home to dolphins, whales and porpoises. I was constantly scanning the ocean surface hoping to see their fins.

We pressed on over some particularly boggy, slippy hills. The day had turned blustery, and the rain had returned. Pedro, Steffen and I were the first of our group to arrive into Castro Urdiales. We were soggy and exhausted. For some reason, that we couldn't fathom, the town was bursting at the seams, people were everywhere. And yet it wasn't a holiday or even the weekend. We definitely didn't have it in us to make it to the next town. I went into full on tour guide mode, doing the rounds of the hostels, to find us beds for the night. There was nothing. Pedro and Steffen walked the extra few kilometres out to the municipal albergue to try their luck there. Pedro secured overflow accommodation for us. In tents! It was our only option. He was extremely chuffed with himself.

The others, when they arrived, had a tepid reaction to Pedro's having saved the day, or rather, the night for us. His mood darkened. He was their saviour, and he thought they should shower him with much more praise and recognition than they were doing. He felt they were underrating him and under-appreciating him. I sighed inwardly. I knew those signs. I sensed a downward spiral coming. I tried to make up for what he mistakenly perceived as their lack of appreciation. It didn't help. It never did.

While I was trying to support Pedro's feelings, Celine scored herself a place within the albergue. No tent for her! How did she do that? She seemed to effortlessly draw to herself everything she needed. She had also got herself a ride to the clinic to sort out her blisters. And then as we were heading out to dinner, I offered her my good rain jacket. What was I thinking? Only that she didn't have one. But now I didn't have one either. We made our way through the lashing rain, Celine snug and dry in my jacket. And me? Soon soaked to the skin.

We were wet and tired and facing a waterlogged, windy night in tents. Except for Celine, of course. Andy soon had us all helpless with laughter with his naturally buoyant good humour. Even Pedro, whose dark moods could last for days, was high on Camino camaraderie while we were all together. But once it was just the two of us, back in our tent, his dark mood descended again. I spent a miserable night sucked into the vortex caused by the clammy tent walls and Pedro's simmering repressed anger. He was sucking the air and the warmth out of the already oppressive atmosphere in the tent. When I woke up, the next morning, stiff, cold and sleep deprived he was hovering over me impatient to be off. He needed no coffee, he was fuelled by his dank, dark mood. Why didn't I just tell him to get over himself and go ahead without me? I could have so easily have had a leisurely breakfast with coffee and caught him up later. Why? It never occurred to me. When the others caught up with us Pedro's demons of the previous night evaporated. What a relief! The rain had abated too, and our damp packs steamed in the gentle morning sunshine.

Chapter 10
THE SINGING TREE

"Sometimes you don't know the value of a moment

until it becomes a memory."

Dr Seuss

Next stop Laredo. We didn't dawdle as we followed the yellow arrows toward the old part of town. We were on the hunt for the convent albergue we had chosen as our home for the night. After the previous night in tents, we wanted to get to it as fast as possible and bagsy our beds. Laredo is a beautiful old town, bearing no relation to its Texan 'tocayo' or namesake. It is a working fishing port and a "leisure" port providing sanctuary to some pretty fancy ocean-going vessels. On our way in we passed swanky apartment complexes as well. The wealthy residents of Bilbao and Santander flock here in the summer.

We powered down its ancient streets looking for our convent albergue. This part of Laredo hadn't been turned into a themed amusement zone for tourists, like so many cities and towns elsewhere in Spain. It was still a very local neighbourhood with washing draped to dry, obscuring the medieval facades. We broke our stride to peek into open doorways with courtyards, crumbling stable doors and fountains. The gothic churches and arches, cobbled alleyways, and the remains of Laredo's 13th century walls would have to wait until after we'd secured our beds. I was looking forward to the Calle del Infierno or Hell Street which led down to the old shipyards. Maybe that's why there seemed to be a great many monasteries, convents and hermitages here, built to counteract the presence of Hell Street.

We arrived at the convent albergue to find the sisters were a nun down. Sister Maria was unwell. They were hard pushed to greet and accommodate the steady flow of pilgrims. So, I stepped in to help with the pilgrim check in. I got to play at hospitalera for a few hours. It was a bit of an eye opener to see how some pilgrims treated the check in as if they were in a 5-star hotel, evidently miffed at being kept waiting. They thought the nuns were there to pander to their every whim and desire, as if the convent was a generic hotel. It was quite sobering seeing how dismissive they were of the nuns' efforts. I noticed this applied particularly to bickering middle-aged couples. They seemed jaded and disinterested in it all. As if they were only walking the Camino to tick it off their bucket list. I hoped that Pedro and I would never fall into that pattern of sniping at each other.

Once I had done my stint as an honorary nun, or at least assistant to the nuns, I tried to remain in what I assumed to be a nun like attitude of gratitude. I was grateful that I had an opportunity to help others. I was grateful for my cold shower in the communal bathroom. Any hot water having long since been used up. By those bickering couples taking individual showers I figured. No hopping in together and sharing the hot water for them. I was grateful for my tiny travel towel as I patted myself 'dry' even though it only seemed to redistribute the moisture on my body rather than actually absorbing it. I was grateful that Pedro and I weren't a bickering middle-aged couple, and I was also grateful that we had our own private cell, complete with the ever-presented oversized crucifix bearing down on us. And while Pedro and the others went off exploring Laredo before we all met up for pre-dinner drinks, I was grateful that I could assist Andy by being his interpreter as he navigated the dreaded Spanish postal system.

When Andy began his Camino, his plan was to have a soulful solitary march across northern Spain, skinning a squirrel for dinner over the campfire before retiring to his hammock strung between two trees to commune with the stars. He had finally given up on that idea. It was now time to send his camping gear back to England. If it is true that the Camino gives you what you need, as opposed to what you might think you want, I guess Andy must have needed less solitude and more company. His Camino had turned into a far more convivial affair than he'd anticipated. He had finally surrendered to, and accepted that. Well, almost. I could tell that he had thought long and hard about it, and it still wasn't easy for him to let go of either his camping gear, or that vision of himself as the lone camper. He puffed anxiously on a ciggy as we wandered down to the post office, just a short walk from the convent. He was evidently having an internal struggle, to actually let go of both his expectations and his equipment. I didn't quite get why it was such a big deal to him. He was simply lugging around a few extra kilos of weight. And a few extra kilos are a big deal when you have to carry it on your back as you walk 800 kms. The only thing I could offer to help him was that he would feel better once he'd done the deed.

But I warned him not to expect it to be easy. Not the psychological letting go, but the actual dispatching of the goods. I explained to him that, unlike the orderly queues and brisk service of an English post office, he could expect long lines and even longer conversations between the locals and the post office staff. The point of such practical interactions in England might be to efficiently and quickly as possible complete the transaction. Whereas in Spain, any interaction, wherever it happened to take place was taken as the opportunity for a good old gossip. He would need to be patient. I could tell he wasn't too happy at the prospect. It was only going to prolong his discomfort, but best he be prepared.

As it happened there was no queue snaking out the door when we got there. There was only one customer in the post office and they were in and out in a matter of seconds. This didn't actually make it any easier for Andy though, quite the reverse, I think. He didn't have time for one last moment with his hammock, tarp and tackle. It was out of his hands and being unceremoniously flung into a cart behind the desk clerk before he had even the slightest chance of changing his mind. You would have thought he was sending his youngest child out on a long journey alone and unprotected. I honestly didn't get what all the fuss was about. The desk clerk was bemused when he turned around to find Andy still standing there staring forlornly at the bundle that had been so unceremoniously dealt with. Before he could lunge across the counter to retrieve the package, I snapped him out of his trance and gently tugged at his elbow to lead him out of the door.

There was only one thing for it. A stiff drink. A beer wouldn't cut it. I scouted out the nearest bar which, being Spain, was two doors away. The choice was obvious. Pacharan. This would be the first time we had drunk our favourite beverage before dinner. And here had been Andy thinking he had come to the Camino del Norte for a walk of lofty ideals, communing with nature, cleansing himself inside and out with pure stream water, no alcohol or other such indulgences. As he came to terms with his new Camino-self I wondered if any of us get the Camino we had envisaged before setting foot on it? Mine was certainly all I had hoped it would be. And then I remembered Sarajevo. Only one more day left before I had to leave.

+++++++++++++++++

I wanted to hit the pause button. Sarajevo was coming up fast on my horizon. The next day passed way too quickly for my liking. I was savouring each step, milking every moment. I tried to imprint every yellow arrow, every sound and every smell on my mind. I was storing them up to enjoy them again in Sarajevo during the endless mind-numbing meetings that awaited me. To replay them as I sat in the stuffy hotel boardroom.

On that last day the Camino gave me a series of seascapes that, if captured in watercolour, you would say the artist had surely exaggerated. The beauty of that day stays with me even now. The cliff faces bounced back the sun's rays and backlit the surfers as they glided through silver tubes to shore. On the last stretch of beach before Santander, I lost myself in the clouds as I followed the water's edge. I have a massive dislike of sand in my shoes and yet I fairly floated along hypnotised by the blurred horizon where the sea and sky blended. I did not think that I would be able to persuade my legs to carry me off the Camino of my own volition. Until I realised that I had already floated myself off the trail. The others had been jumping up and down shouting at me as they saw me go blindly past the marker pointing the way to the ferry. I had to turn around and retrace two kms.

In Santander we enjoyed a leisurely three-course lunch in a local restaurant away from all the tourists. By mid-afternoon rain had set in and we were full up and drowsy. We still had a way to go to get to the albergue that Celine had earmarked for the night, run by a French woman. It was meant to be pretty special. None of us felt inclined to tromp through the city outskirts in the rain. There was a taxi stand right at the exit of the restaurant. We gravitated as a group towards it and bagged ourselves a couple of cabs. I made sure to have the taxis drop us off well out of eyesight of the albergue. By now I was barely hanging on by my fingertips to the bottom rung of the perfect pilgrim scale.

On this, my last evening, I slipped outside the albergue to take in the sunset to add yet another magical memory to my store. I stood and focused intently on the moment. The sun heading homewards, slanting, just so, to illuminate a giant fir tree, from whose branches starlings were exuberantly singing the day to a close. Suddenly, as if they could no longer contain the joy of their song they erupted into the sky like a feathered firework. There was such a surfeit of beauty on this Camino, I was spoilt by it, and I knew I was lucky because I couldn't take it for granted. I was about to have it wrenched from my grasp for 5 whole days. That made me appreciate it all even more fiercely. It occurred to me that this could be a 'Camino lesson' of which I should take note. "Fiercely appreciate each day, however ordinary it might seem on the surface." In my daily life, before the Camino, I used to take so much for granted. Do realisations like this have an expiry date? Once I get to Santiago will I just go back to the way I was, under-appreciating my life? Or do they stick around and change me forever? And will I know? If they stick around, I'll know, I thought as I drank in the sound of the starlings singing the day to a close.

I went back inside to see if I could claw back a few points on the perfect pilgrim scale. I offered to help with the dinner preparations. There was a feast! Mixed salad, tortilla, pumpkin soup, roasted vegetables. I was laying the delicious food out on the tables as the first pilgrims arrived to take their places. I recognised the faces of the feuding couples from the albergue in Laredo. They didn't seem to have been infused with the Camino spirit in the interim. As they pushed their chairs back from the table, I heard a few mutterings about the lack of meat. They swept in and out without even a cursory offer of helping to prepare or clear away dinner. Still, another Camino rule is not to judge, and I was very certain we would have been heavily judged by them for arriving by taxi. Our little crew swung into action, washing the dishes and wiping down the tables. Steffen, on the other hand, got a right old telling off from me for expecting us to pick up his dishes. I snapped a teacloth at him. I told him to get his arse up and help, I wasn't his mother, he wasn't a child, and I wasn't there to serve him, he could bloody well pull his weight. He meekly adopted a position at the sink, dishes done, he then dried every last knife, fork and spoon. I had expected him to tell me to sod off, but he seemed to almost like being told off. He was in his early twenties and single. It was just downright odd that he wasn't off looking for company his own age and, well, not to put too fine a point on it, maybe even the chance to get laid.

The next morning, I looked with great fondness at the heads popping up from their sleeping bags around the dormitory. I loved and appreciated each one of them. Even Steffen. I knew that I would very soon be sleeping in high thread count cotton sheets, luxuriating in coffee in bed, taking a steaming power shower and wrapping myself in a sheet-sized fluffy bath towel. I would have exchanged all that in a heartbeat for the nights I would be missing of tepid showers in communal bathrooms and blotting myself dry on my stamp sized chamois leather of a travel towel. Then walking 10 kms before morning coffee.

Despite my efforts to stop time, the dreaded morning had come. The one on which I had to tear myself away from this Camino cocoon of love, laughter and light. I actually had to turn my back on my Camino family and walk in the opposite direction. How would I even find my way without the yellow arrows to guide me?

Chapter 11
BLAH, BLAH. BLAH

"Come quickly. You mustn't miss the dawn. It will never be just like this again."

Georgia O'Keeffe

A white owl glided past me in the pre-dawn light. I watched it for a long time, feeling that it was a sign meant just for me. For this morning. As this was the morning that I was leaving the Camino. I wanted to keep its memory with me as I negotiated the complex series of trains, buses and planes that would take me to Sarajevo. My Camino family accompanied me to the Santander railway station. They deposited me, with hugs and kisses, on the platform. And turned and walked in the opposite direction with barely a backward glance. As my train approached, it took a massive effort of will for me not to run after them. But I forced myself to climb aboard. Now it was just me and Boris sitting forlornly in a corner of the train carriage. Out the window I could see their backpacks receding into the distance.

Bereft is not too strong a word to describe how I felt as the train rewound the kilometres of the Camino back to Bilbao. I went to the Post Office. There, waiting for me, was my travelling case I'd packed, all that time ago in Granada. My smart red Samsonite. It would now replace Boris as my travelling companion. Boris I stored in the basement of an Airbnb flat I had rented for the night. He looked balefully back at me from his dungeon. I felt exactly the same way and was very sorely tempted to say sod it to Sarajevo, scoop him back up and start walking in the direction of Santander, again.

Back in my civvies, thoroughly showered, hair blow dried and straightened. And with a touch of mascara, I didn't recognise myself as I stared in the mirror. I wondered what would happen if I turned up at the 5-star hotel in Sarajevo, mud spattered and stinky, with Boris on my back. "No more thinking that way." I reprimanded myself. I was a good girl, I played by the rules. And I would arrive at the spiffy 5-star hotel as the professional woman they expected me to be. As always.

I took in my first glimpses of the city on the short taxi ride from the airport. My attention is always drawn to words, even if I have no clue how to decipher them. And so, as the taxi driver navigated our route through the beautiful Sarajevo valley to the hotel, I noticed that the road signs hadn't been translated from Bosnian into English for my comfort. I loved that. It didn't feel as if this country, Bosnia-Herzegovina, had twisted itself into uncomfortable contortions to conform to a more easily digestible version of itself just to suit the tourist industry. It all felt a little raw, edgy and interesting. And even in my funk at being there, I had to admit that Sarajevo was visually stunning.

At the hotel I applied my game face, along with my mascara, and got ready to brave the hours of discussion ahead. I greeted my colleagues with air kisses all round and endured the arrival dinner. Despite my gruelling journey that had begun before dawn and included three changes of plane, going to bed was still not an option. Sadly, no Camino curfew was in place here. Staying up until the wee hours was a required component of these work meetings. And it was very much frowned upon if you were not a 'team player' and didn't partake with gusto in the after-dinner festivities. I, of course, complied. At last, I ticked off my first night away from the Camino, I couldn't wait to see the remaining days count down to zero.

The next morning and every morning in Sarajevo, I got up at dawn to run. Even though I had only had a couple of hours' sleep, I forced myself up and out of bed. That early morning fresh air and physical exercise gave me the strength of mind and body to endure the hours that awaited me in the overheated conference room. I couldn't have done without it. It was so odd not to be following yellow arrows. I found myself constantly on the lookout for them. I love exploring new cities as they stir themselves blearily from their beds, before they too have their game faces in place. As a city comes to, I feel as if I can connect more directly with its essence. Before lipstick has been applied, as shutters are rattled awake, streets hosed down, and scraggy cats clatter the lids off dustbins. There is something vulnerable and revealing about a city at this hour.

After breakfast, along with 'my team', I dutifully followed the signs down to the hotel's conference facilities. We were looking for the 'Adriatic Suite'. The word 'Adriatic' suggested exotic beaches and sunshine. I was sure the hotel chain's marketing team had held protracted discussions before they'd conjured up that fanciful name to lure us into the dank, dark dungeon that was the hotel basement. No point in wasting scenic views on prisoners like us. The 'Adriatic Suite' had been purposefully designed to suck any joy and spontaneity out of us. It was the antithesis of the Camino in every respect, no sunlight, no fresh air, no beauty.

And so, I braved the long hours. I followed the prompts and played my role repeating the same requests, suggesting the same changes, offering the same solutions that I had done the previous year in Athens, the year before that in Tel Aviv and the year prior to that in Palermo. I appreciated how lucky I was to get to travel to such destinations, I really did. It was just that most of the time I might as well have been in the middle of any conference room, in any hotel, in any generic town centre, anywhere in the world. Hour upon hour of blah blah blah. So many words used - so little actually being said. I flowed with the flow charts. I focused intently on the newly formed focus groups. I slid into the sales funnels. I dug deep into my well of resolve willing my face to assume the appearance of someone fascinated by all the financial projections.

Time took on a different dimension in the 'Adriatic Suite'. I was tempted to call the technical support department to complain that the clock on the wall, although loudly ticking our lives away, wasn't working properly. Its hands didn't appear to be moving. It was like a roulette wheel stuck in place by a ball jammed in its mechanism. I had floated into the room on a little wisp of rose-tinted cloud that I had picked up from my sunrise run. It had detached itself and slid out under the door leaving me alone. It was no match for the mind-numbing might of the itemised agenda, nor the vast expanse of white damask tablecloths covering the tables around the room. The sheer volume of white trapped and smothered any last vestige of joy that had survived the descent into the basement.

Even the fruit laid out for us was visibly decaying under the glare of the overhead strip lighting. No living thing can thrive for long down here, I mused. Every bit of residual vitality will inevitably atrophy before that itemised schedule reaches 'any other business' or even more cruelly, 'blue sky thinking'. In the corner of the room, on its own white island, lurked an electric urn. It, occasionally, grumbled, steamed and hissed, as if in contempt at some particularly inane remark issued from around the conference table. There were no freshly prepared steaming cups of cafe con leche for me here in the 'Adriatic Suite'. Only gallons of tepid rancid brown liquid.

I was reminded of another time and another malodorous coffee urn. I let my mind off the leash and reminisced about my days temping in offices as a teenager in the summer holidays. I remembered the shoulder padded power-suited staff swishing past me, self-importantly clutching files to their chests, entering the sacred realm of the conference room. I wanted to join them and take part in the dynamic world changing discussions that they were obviously having behind the door they closed. But that was not to be. I was left to tend the coffee urn in the kitchen and only enter the hallowed ground to dispense its vile contents. Contemplating this, it occurred to me that I should have been more careful about what I had wished for back then. And as I gazed at the vast expanse of white around me, I wondered if I had made any other wishes that had yet to come true and were stealthily getting ready to trip me up.

Finding Love On The Camino

As I was waiting for the others to join me in the lobby for the group dinner that night, I stepped outside the hotel to get some fresh air. We were right in the centre of the city. A tour guide was showing her group the "Sarajevo roses". Sarajevo roses are scars in the concrete made by the explosions of mortar shells during the Siege of Sarajevo in the Bosnian War that raged here between 1992 and 1995. These scars have been filled in with red resin and left as memorials to the fallen. We had watched this war 'live' on the telly. I remember my reaction, a mixture of horror, impotence and disbelief. The guide gave a comprehensive overview of the facts and figures of the war that had decimated this city and its population. She competently and professionally rendered it into a digestible wikipedia version. Most of the group looked uncomfortable, I could sense them hoping that no one would be insensitive enough to ask a question on this traumatic subject. As I knew, and I'm sure the guide did too, there will always be someone who wants to know more, poke a finger into unbearably deep and private wounds. To have their morbid fascination satisfied. I watched that hand go up. Then I remembered my Camino lesson number two; mine is not to judge. My colleagues joined me on the pavement, and we headed to dinner.

When they politely enquired about my Camino. I couldn't explain to them the enormity of my experience and how bonded I felt to my Camino family. I tried, but they rolled their eyes and pointed out that I had only known these people for less than ten days. All I could think was that, although we all worked for a travel company, they hadn't experienced the same intensity of travel, particularly as youngsters, as I had. Your emotions and experiences are heightened by unfamiliar landscapes and exotic surroundings. Meeting new friends as you sleep on rat infested train stations or by being thrown into each other's laps in sleeping compartments of express trains. Or trekking up mountains together, surviving freak snowstorms, malaria and altitude sickness. And then you are suddenly saying goodbye. In that moment you want to swear lifelong friendship. But you simply hug and wave them off. And in the upcoming days, those storm proof bonds that tied you, gradually slacken until you drift completely apart. Oceans of years and experiences coming between you. You will never know if those dreams they shared with you came true. It always felt unbearably sad to me. Was a Camino family different from this? I hoped so. I hoped we would always be a family. I found goodbyes too gut wrenching. But maybe I was getting ahead of myself in my eagerness to be bonded to my new friends.

But bonded I certainly was. And it was all so unexpected. It was maybe strange that it hadn't occurred to me that Pedro and I might form our own Camino family. Of course, I knew all about the phenomenon. It just hadn't been something that I'd thought that we would get to experience. Being such a self-contained couple. Sure, I had thought we would get to meet some nice people along the way and have some good chats, but I had never envisaged us walking as part of a group. In fact, originally when we had discussed my coming to Sarajevo, he had said that he would probably hole up for those few days in, or near to, Bilbao until I returned. He wanted us to walk the whole Camino together. I hadn't reminded him of that before I left. I wanted him to enjoy the companionship of our new friends.

I found it so interesting that 'fate' would have placed us all together on the path at the same time. Had that car share ride been a day or two either side of our departure date we would very probably never have met them. Had any one of them made just a slight alteration to their plans we wouldn't be walking together. Was it all just random chance? Or was there actually a divine plan behind it all? I could see how both these theories could be true. The former an easy belief to accommodate. The latter a little less so. But to a universe that orchestrated the seamless co-existence of entire galaxies at one end of the scale, and the functioning of the intricate inner galaxies of our bodies, at the other end of the scale, surely such a concept would be child's play. To line up a few individuals, in Spain, at a certain time. Whatever the answer ,I could see how I had already benefited from my time with each of them. Particularly Diola and Celine.

I had been immediately and viscerally drawn to Diola. And she had more than lived up to my expectations of her being a great person to spend time with. She was so calm and sure of herself. She and her family had had an unimaginably tough time in Africa, before settling into a comfortable, well regulated, satisfying life in Germany. Despite the hardships she had suffered, she laughed easily and took great joy in the world around her. People naturally gravitated to her. And it just felt soothing to be in her presence. I wondered if it was precisely because she'd had to overcome so many obstacles at such a young age that she had become so self-assured and appreciative of what she had. I really looked forward to getting back to the Camino so I could get to know her even more.

And I was totally in awe of Celine. She was spontaneous and totally unselfconscious. She hadn't even walked a proper path from her home town before joining up with the Camino. She hadn't let that stand in her way in the least. Even the fact that she was pretty low on funds didn't deter her. She absolutely expected everything and everyone to pander to her needs. And they did. Including me. She didn't seem to manipulate things. It just naturally happened. And both these women had chosen to walk alone, so fearlessly. They hadn't given it a second thought. I found that astonishing. Both were younger than me but had a lot to teach me in terms of my self-confidence. I thanked either the chance happenstance, or the orchestrated maneuvrings of the universe, for placing me in the company of such strong, independent women on the Camino. I didn't really care which it was. I was just so happy that it had.

The Camino WhatsApp chat, that we had set up to communicate with each other, hummed and pinged. I was an outsider looking in. That sucked. There was talk of gatherings for pre-dinner drinks, albergues to consider, Sarah and Richard were off to a wedding in England, they promised to catch up with us on their return. And even surfing lessons on a free afternoon. My phone was full up with messages from the group, but none from Pedro. I found that strange. I thought he would call to find out how I was doing in Sarajevo. I was securing our income for the next 12 months. I rang him many times. But got through only once. And when I did, he was impatient with me. He wanted to get back to the group. He didn't even try to hide his disinterest in what I was doing. His irritation was palpable. I got it. I really did. He was having fun and I was spoiling his Camino buzz by talking about work. But I started to get an uneasy feeling that something wasn't as it should be. I couldn't keep that feeling at bay, an ever-increasing sense of insecurity. It came in waves. Even though things weren't fireworks between us, I never doubted our commitment to each other. And I was here working for us.

Five tough days later I released Boris from his cell in Bilbao, we were delighted to be reunited with each other. I could barely wait to see everyone. The reunion was to take place in a town called Villaviciosa. I don't think the literal translation is actually vicious town but in my current state of insecurity and anxiety the name made me even more uneasy. Pedro knew what time my bus was arriving, and the bus terminal was just a 10 minute walk away from the albergue they had chosen for the night. I was looking forward to his familiar tap on my shoulder as I bent over to retrieve Boris from the luggage hold under the bus. No shoulder tap came. The call of a beer or two had evidently drowned out any voice prompting him to come and greet me. Boris and I accompanied each other to the albergue where everyone was gathered. Andy, Diola and Celine jumped up in excitement and happiness to see me. Steffen, they said, had hooked up with a younger crowd and was off surfing. Good for him! I thought. Pedro, eventually, put down his beer and came over to greet me. He gave me a limp hug. Not good. Maybe my feelings of insecurity were well founded after all. I couldn't ignore it. Something was wrong. I forced him to one side to talk with me. I knew that he hated confrontation and would more than likely just clam up. And that's what he did. He simply refused to talk to me.

Pedro had chosen that night's restaurant. It was an authentic sidreria, a cider bar. But a very high-class establishment with corresponding high class prices. No doubt worth every penny, but some of our group were on very tight budgets. Pedro knew this and yet he had chosen the expensive restaurant and expected everyone to congratulate and thank him for his great choice. It didn't happen. The others took the perfectly reasonable decision to have one drink at the cider bar and move on.

They were not beholden to him. Faced with the prospect of sitting with my husband in stony silence I jumped ship too. I don't know who was more surprised that I dared to do that, Pedro or me.

I went with the others, and we found a lovely, lively little place. We were about to tuck into a delicious meal when Pedro turned up. He begrudgingly acknowledged what a good place it was. He seemed surprised that we had found such a gem without his guidance. He was soon all laughter and Mr Congeniality again. But as soon as we entered our double room at the albergue his smile was automatically extinguished. He became stony faced and got immediately into bed. He turned as far away as he could possibly get from me without falling off the bed. All night I was buffeted by pounding waves of repressed anger coming from his rigid form.

Chapter 12

THE FORK IN THE ROAD

"You choose which track you will head down, toward breakdown or breakthrough."

Yogi Berra

The following morning, I woke up feeling decidedly ropey. I was feeling the effects of my long trip from Sarajevo the day before. Plus a night with little sleep. Oh, and also my ill-advised attempt to jolly myself along, in the face of Pedro's indifference, with one too many Pacharans. Even so my heart gave a little leap. I was no longer in Sarajevo. I was actually here on the Camino! With a day of walking ahead of me. I could imagine nothing better. There was absolutely nowhere else in the world I'd rather be. Pedro's side of the bed was empty. I could see his phone on the bedside table and his backpack in the corner. Well at least he hadn't gone on ahead without me. Blimey, if Pedro was up already, maybe the others were too. I'd better get a move on.

The turn off to the Camino Primitivo was coming up fast.

I went downstairs to the breakfast room to grab a quick coffee before reassembling Boris. This was a big day for us. The Camino Primitivo awaited! Pedro and I had intended from the get-go, even before we had left Granada, only to follow the Camino del Norte until we reached the Camino Primitivo, and then we were going to walk the inland Camino Primitivo to Santiago de Compostela, the official end of the Camino. The others were all up for this plan too. I was anxious they might be ready to set off. Phew! I needn't have worried. I walked in and found Diola, Celine and Andy huddled together over their coffee, deep in discussion. Good, they didn't have their packs with them, so they obviously weren't ready to go either. Diola pulled back a chair and signalled for me to join them. They all looked a little serious. None of the usual pre-walk banter and laughter with which our days usually began. I looked around the table trying to gauge from their expressions what was up. No one met my eye. Diola cleared her throat. Rather ominously. But still didn't actually speak. Evidently reluctant to say whatever it was she was about to say. This made me shift uncomfortably in my chair. What on earth was going on? Whatever it was, the others were obviously in on it. And given the fact that they were looking anywhere rather than at me, it was clear that whatever it was she was about to say, they knew I wasn't going to like it. What the hell? This was not how I had envisaged my first morning back on the Camino. My mind ran through a series of possible scenarios; something bad had happened to Pedro, but surely, they would have come to find me right away? Something was wrong with one of them - but other than looking shifty they all looked perfectly fine. One of them had received bad news and had to leave? I certainly hoped not!

At last, Diola spoke. She told me that she had decided not to walk the challenging Camino Primitivo. She wanted to continue walking the Camino del Norte to the end of the Camino. She said she was really, really sorry but she had already found the walking tough going, harder than she had thought she would. She hadn't slept all night worrying about the Primitivo and wondering if she was physically up for it. She said she knew she wasn't. Shit. So, it was none of the options that had occurred to me. Instead, our Camino family was breaking up. Without Diola, things wouldn't be the same at all.

But she hadn't finished talking yet. The ominous throat clearing began again. I felt the absurd urge to stick my fingers in my ears and go 'la la la can't hear you!' as you do as a child when you don't want to hear what someone has to say. I was already reeling from her first bombshell. Whatever it was she had to add, I definitely did not want to hear it. I gripped the sides of my chair and steeled myself for the worst. Though I couldn't really see how much worse it could get than the dissolution of our family. As it happened it could. And not just a little. Much worse. Having made her decision this morning, Celine and Andy had decided to walk the less arduous route with her. That shouldn't have surprised me. Last night, before their very eyes, Pedro and I had morphed into the dreaded middle-age bickering couple. The thought of walking with us would have made their decision really easy.

When I had entered the breakfast room and found them with their heads together, talking conspiratorially, they had in fact been making their plans for the Norte. I had guessed that Diola held the superpower of bending others to her will. Now she had more than proved it. They had just been texting Sarah and Richard when I came in. They had replied that they were happy to go along with whatever the majority of the group decided. Which left Pedro and me to walk the Primitivo route on our own. Maybe with Steffen, maybe not. He was still missing in action. I was absolutely gutted. Our Camino family was disintegrating before my very eyes. I would quite literally have given anything for that not to happen. My mind just didn't want to take it in, and I found myself thinking that maybe this was all just a really bad nightmare, that maybe I'd wake up in a minute. But it wasn't and I didn't. This shit was really happening. And there was nothing I could do to stop it. Unless…

Pedro really had his heart set on walking the Camino Primitivo. Knowing him as I did, I could not see him changing his mind. I knew that if he thought I wanted to go with the others on the Camino del Norte he would dig his heels in and refuse to agree to a change in plan. Particularly given his present mood. I knew that I was most definitely not the person to approach him. But I did know who the right person was, Diola. She said she was more than happy to give it her very best shot. But given how much Pedro had spoken about the wonders of the Primitivo and how much he was looking forward to it, she doubted very much that she could convince him. She hugged me and went off to look for him.

Celine and Andy, their decisions already made, went off to finish their packing and focus on their day ahead. I was left alone. I knew I should be getting organised too, I hadn't showered or packed. But there was no way I could concentrate on those things. I was both dreading, and longing for Diola to return with Pedro's decision. I became aware of the hospitalero hovering at my elbow, obviously wanting to clear the breakfast things off our table. Wanting to get on with his busy day. For him this was just another morning in this Camino town, same old same old. I envied him his complacency. I couldn't face going to my room.

I stood up and cleared our cups and plates to the counter and then, on tenterhooks, I paced up and down the breakfast room. I didn't know what to do with myself. I went over the conversation we had just had. Andy and Celine had quickly sided with Diola rather than with Pedro and me. I had loved my talks and time with each of them; and I thought the feeling had been mutual. I had assumed that they would be at least a little sad to part ways with Pedro and me. Had Andy and Celine aligned with Diola because they didn't want to be stuck with a feuding couple? Had Pedro and I really become one of those dissatisfied, bickering "toxic" couples that I had witnessed in the albergue in Laredo. If that was true, I could understand their reaction. I wouldn't want to walk with one of those either. Or maybe it was just me they had an issue with. Maybe they didn't like my company. Maybe I'm too uptight for them. Too controlling. Just not much fun to be with. It quite literally made me feel sick to the stomach to contemplate this. But once that thought had occurred to me, I couldn't shake it. I recalled a book I had read about a woman walking the Camino with a group of women who, one by one, started to avoid her finally leaving her to walk alone. She couldn't see why. But everyone else could. Oh my God. Was I like her??

I couldn't pace within those walls any longer. I stepped outside the front door. Shit. I could see Pedro and Diola on the terrace of a cafe just the other side of the square. They were deep in conversation, unaware that I was watching them. I could glean no visual clues as to the probable outcome of their discussion; no vigorous nodding or shaking of heads, nothing to suggest which way the conversation was going. I had blithely assumed that Diola would want to persuade Pedro to walk with them. Was she really doing that? Or was she just going through some sort of pretence at trying to persuade him? I parked those thoughts. Hopefully I was completely wrong.

Hang on, they'd just got up and given each other a big hug. Was that a gesture of goodbye and good luck? Or was it - I'm happy you're coming with us? Diola started back across the square in her usual unhurried way. When she caught sight of me her face broke into one of her dazzling smiles. It could only mean one thing. We were all walking the Camino del Norte together. Phew! What a massive relief.

I could have skipped the whole way to Santiago over hot coals. Despite a stonking hangover and little sleep, I glided up one of the steepest sections of the Camino. I barely registered the kilometres flying by. I was on a wave of euphoria, loving and blessing every cow, every hill, every apple tree. And given that we were now in the province of Asturias that was a hell of a lot of trees. If I could only bottle that as a hangover cure, I would be a very rich woman indeed. Diola said Pedro had been quick to capitulate. That amused me. He obviously didn't like the prospect of walking the Primitivo, alone with me. He might actually have had to talk to me.

As we approached the perfect lunch stop - everything about that day was perfect as far as I was concerned - a strikingly pretty, young German girl approached us and immediately asked where Pedro was. He was seated with a far younger group of Mexican guys. I felt a slight tinge of embarrassment on his behalf. They were surely only being polite to him. Fast approaching 50, he was almost twice their age. He ignored me so I left him to it. I hoped they wouldn't take off without him, leaving me to deal with his even fouler mood. I texted him via our WhatsApp chat, telling him where we were headed and letting him know that his accommodation was already paid for. He eventually turned up with the young crowd and they proceeded to frolic like the youngsters they were, well, all bar one.

We were staying at a swanky campsite for the night. We pilgrims were tucked away in a corner, far from the regular holidaymakers. We had our own repurposed utility shed with bunks and a tiny kitchen, perfectly adequate. I happily bagsied myself a bunk and headed to the showers. Pilgrims got to use the same showers as the rest of the holiday makers. They were the sort that had the water flow on a timer. Using them was like doing 'The Bump', an ungainly dance from the disco '80's. You raised your hands in the air and bumped your hips with your dancing partner in time to the music. In the shower version of the dance, you stand under the flow of water, with you hip, back or bum, depending on your height, rhythmically bumping up against the shower knob to keep the water flowing. Your hands, of course, are otherwise engaged with the whole soaping, hair washing thing. In Diola's case she was probably doing 'the Bump' with her knee and in my case, it was a spot halfway up my back.

The following morning Celine, Diola, Andy and I went over to the bar where they were just starting to gear up for the pilgrim breakfast crowd. The bar was in that limbo state, just waking up to the day ahead, with last night's revelries still hanging in the air. Empty beer bottles were being cleared from the tables; spillages wiped up. The coffee machine was starting to huff and blow into action. The aroma coming from it was winning out over the smell of stale beer. We girls were going to buy Andy's breakfast. It was the least we could do for him.

The night before, he had insisted on staying behind in the laundry room and doing the washing while we went on to dinner. All our walking gear fitted into one machine and one drier. Andy insisted there was no point in more than one person being there to oversee it. He said that having brought up four kids by himself it was so much part of his daily routine he would barely notice it.

As I was at the bar getting Andy's breakfast order, Pedro came in and sat down at our table. He took his place expecting me to go back to the bar and bring him his coffee and breakfast. Enough, I thought, he can get his own breakfast. I sat down, enjoyed my coffee and ignored him. This little act of rebellion was so out of character for me. Over our breakfast Diola and I raised the option with the others of renting a flat through Airbnb for a change. There were 3 points in Airbnbs favour we explained to them. 1. We didn't have to worry about 'Completo' or "Full" signs. 2. I didn't have to worry about the frequent gluten fests that were the communal albergue dinners. And 3. When we split the cost between the eight of us, it was even cheaper than staying in albergues. I, myself, had some misgivings about this being appropriate pilgrim procedure but everyone thought it a good idea and so I put my doubts to one side. Everyone set off walking and I stayed behind and found us a great flat in our next town, Gijon. I let everyone know the address on the group WhatsApp chat.

I got walking keeping my eye on the WhatsApp chat making sure everyone got the Airbnb address. Pedro was the only one who didn't respond. I called his phone, but he didn't pick up. I tried repeatedly but I didn't get a response. I was worried he might have lost his phone. Without it he wouldn't know where the Airbnb was. I began to get anxious. How would he get in touch with us? Should I run up ahead and look for him? Was he OK? He didn't even have any money on him. How would he cope? I fretted and fussed. As I caught up with Andy, Diola, and Celine I was hugely relieved to see a message from him appear in the group chat. I eagerly read the group message. "Hi guys! Miss you! Will probably catch up with you all tomorrow. Going surfing!" Thank goodness he was OK. He was off playing with the kids. What a relief!

Once that relief had settled down, the dismay took over. He knew perfectly well how worried I would be about him. He should have rung me straight away instead of ignoring my messages. But I put that aside. I was on a secret mission. I had scoped out the hiking stores that might be available to us in such a big town like Gijon. There was a little something I wanted to get Celine. I love nothing more than surprising people with gifts that I know will be well received and truly welcome. So, we all piled into a Decathlon outdoor store. Celine's backpack was hopelessly outdated and giving her back problems. She needed a new one. I knew I could wave my magic wand and make those issues disappear in a flash. She was a bit tight on funds and didn't have the available cash to do it herself. I've been there. We all have. While Andy was buying new hiking socks, and Diola was stocking up on medical supplies, I called her over to the backpack section and picked out a cousin of Boris's. I told her to pop it on to see how a decent pack felt compared to hers. The look on her face said it all. That's when I said, "C'mon on then, let's take him with us." Her jaw dropped in surprise. Before she could raise any objections, I waved my credit card, which was sort of the same as a magic wand, and the bag was in the bag. Celine lit up like a kid on Christmas morning. She was touched and delighted and didn't hold back in her expression of those feelings. She gave me a massive bear hug. I don't know who was happier.

When I got settled into the Airbnb flat in Gijon my dismay with Pedro from earlier in the day swooped back at me again. I picked up my phone and punched in his number. I didn't really expect him to answer. But he surprised me by picking up. I expected remorse and reassurance. But he gave a blithe 'hola' acting as if nothing were wrong. They say there are moments that change your life. Well, this was mine. Would I play along as I had done for 19 years? Or would I tell him what I was feeling? I tried to bite back my harsh words, as I always had, but there were too many. And so, I told him how I felt. The pent up hurt I had been feeling for 19 years blurted out of me. "How would you feel if I'd taken off without letting you know where I was? How would you feel if I hadn't answered any of your calls? How would you feel if I'd let you know in a group chat that I'd 'catch up with you at some point'?"

He was silent for a few seconds. I wasn't sure what was coming next. Which way would he play it? Would he hang up on me? Then come back, shame faced a few days later knowing that all would be forgiven. Would he apologise to me, calling me Kiki, his pet name for me, and say he was on his way home?

As it turned out. None of the above. Instead, he screamed at me in a crazed tone I had never heard from him before. That he wasn't listening to this. And that he never would again. That he'd had enough. That we were through. That it was over between us.

And with that, he hung up.

Chapter 13
THE END OF THE ROAD

'You will never see the end if you give up in the middle"

Joyce Meyer

I sat on the floor. The phone still in my hand. Unable to move. Pedro's words "Ya esta! Ya terminamos!" reverberating through me, "We're through!". My mind objectively knew he had said those words, but the rest of me was having a hard time catching up. I was numb. I thought that if I didn't move, if I stayed very, very, very still, time would stop.

I was surrounded by a sea of beige. A beige couch on a beige carpet held within beige walls. 'Mi Casa es tu Casa!' empty words to me, "My home is your home". Those words stared down at me from their beige frame over the beige couch. I was in the Airbnb in Gijon. Before that phone call this living room had seemed so luxurious. Now it was just bland. Beige and bland. All the life gone out of it. I had just had the most personal conversation of my life in the most impersonal surroundings.

I didn't want to think. If only I could just stay here forever, in this sea of blandness, feeling nothing and thinking nothing. I stayed seated on the floor, my back against the beige couch. With the phone still in my hand. In exactly the same position. I tried to hold back the floodgate. But I couldn't. Thoughts began spewing into my mind. What did his words imply? What the hell was I supposed to do now? I had not seen this coming. Absolutely everything had lined up for our walking this Camino together. It was so obviously meant to be. This was the way forward for us. This was a consolidation of our relationship. This was a consolidation of our love for each other. That was what this whole Camino was about. A new beginning.

Wasn't it?

Or was this just one big ball of denial on my part. Could everyone else see that but me? Had all our mutual friends and family been thinking when is she going to realise what's going on? When the hell is she going to wake up? Was even my Camino family thinking that too? Damn it! I'd focused so much on NOT being like my mum. I'd even purposefully deepened my voice so as not to sound like her. She had a light, high pitched, little girl lost voice. She had always been looking to be rescued. Going from one man to the next. Always looking for a knight on a white charger to save her. I wasn't like that. I was the strong independent one. I could save myself thank you very much. I was the one people turned to in order to be saved.

Was that the problem? Had I been involved in some sick game all along? Was I jumping in and saving people when I was secretly desperate to be saved myself? Silently screaming, save me, rescue me! It's my turn now. Was I hoping to cure him so that he would, in turn, cure me? Was I mirroring the need within me to be saved, projecting that out on to him? But I still loved him. I was the only one who could see through his moods and understand him. Who else would?

I continued just sitting there in that bland, beige room aware that the light was growing dimmer. Time hadn't stopped still. It had kept going. In the outer world the day was drawing to a close. I slowly became peripherally aware of life going on around me. Just outside the living room window I could hear the sounds of the neighbours going about their daily lives. It was the end of the working day. TVs were being switched on. Kids were being yelled at to come in for their dinner. Cars' doors slammed as people returned home from work. Couldn't they tell a bomb had just gone off in their midst? Couldn't they feel the shock waves rippling through the walls?

A torrent of thoughts kept surging through me. They went round and round in circles. Careening blindly, getting nowhere. I kept thinking how I still loved him, at least, how I thought I still loved him. Did I? Was that true? Or had that well run dry? Had he just sucked the last drop of love out of me? And then how on earth would he get by without me? He would have no one to save him from himself. No one to rescue him from his dark moods. And is it possible that he really no longer loved me? How could that be true? He had sacrificed everything to be with me here in Spain. His career, his country, his family. What was I going to do now about the rest of my bloody life?

We had planned this Camino together. Did I even want to walk it now without him? How could I carry on? How could I go to all those places we had talked about? To experience all that beauty alone without him. What would be the point of it? And then arriving at the cathedral square in Santiago without Pedro holding my hand would be wretched. Literally unbearable. No, I couldn't do that.

There was a scraping sound. What was that sound? It must be chairs on the kitchen floor. Diola, Celine and Andy had been in the kitchen. They were still in there now talking in hushed tones. They were obviously aware of the shouted conversation that had just taken place in the living room. What was I going to tell them? After that call I certainly didn't expect to be part of the Camino family. The Camino? What was I going to do about the Camino? I couldn't continue walking with them after this. I couldn't inflict myself upon them. It was out of the question. I couldn't stick those kind, generous people with the weeping, wailing woman I knew, at any moment now, I was going to become. I needed to work my shit out alone. They were, right now, getting ready for another fun evening on the Camino. They were making plans for dinner. No way would I suck all the joy out of their Camino. That much was obvious to me.

So, I had a decision to make. I either needed to go home or I needed to walk alone. Either way would be gut wrenching. But I knew there were no other options available to me. Walking alone. I knew I could never do that. That wasn't me. I wasn't up for that. It just felt too sad, lonely and terrifying to contemplate. I didn't have the strength for it. So that left the other option. Go home. I chose 'go home'. Boris and I would go to the train station the next day and begin the journey back to Granada.

I continued to sit there. The yellow arrows faded from view. Where would my path be now?

Chapter 14

MONDAY NIGHT FEVER

"Oh no not I, I will survive

Oh as long as I know how to love, I know I'll stay alive

I've got all my life to live

And I've got all my love to give and I'll survive

I will survive"

Gloria Gaynor

So, my mind was made up. I was going home. I was leaving the Camino. Again, I heard the scraping of chairs on the kitchen floor. And I heard footsteps approaching the door that separated me from Andy, Celine and Diola. I didn't move. I sat on that beige carpet in that bland room willing them not to knock on the door. Willing them not to come in to see if 'I was all right.'

Pedro hadn't called back to say he was sorry, to say that he hadn't meant it when he'd told me that our marriage was over. And I knew perfectly well that he wasn't going to. There was no reprieve for me. No Camino miracle. Boris and I were leaving. We were going home to

Granada, alone, to work out what-the-hell-I-was-going-to-do-with-the-rest-of-my-life.

The knock on the door came.

Diola and Celine entered first. Andy was hovering behind. Instinctively he was letting the women pick up the pieces of me from that beige carpet. I let Diola's long arms wrap around me but felt no comfort. She gently pulled me up and told me to come with them into the kitchen. I obeyed her, damn that woman had powers of persuasion.

They took their seats on one side of the kitchen table. Diola sat me down opposite them. I began to cry. Why did this feel like an intervention? I tried to cry quietly. It was the least I could do for them. I didn't want to make a fuss. I didn't want to ruin their evening.

Andy was spokesperson. "OK, so we heard what went on in there," he said slowly and gently. "Firstly, we want to make it very, very clear to you that your husband is being a total arsehole. Secondly, we know you, and that you're going to want to take off by yourself because you don't want to spoil our Camino. But we don't accept that. We want you to continue the Camino with us. You can be by yourself. Walk alone. Cry all you want. Whatever you need to do. You have our unconditional support and acceptance. But we're not letting you go through this alone."

That did it. I couldn't pull myself together. I couldn't plaster a fake smile on my face. I couldn't pick myself up and apologise for all the fuss I was making. I wanted to, desperately. I wanted to tell them I was fine! Part of me knew that was the right thing to do. But there was another part of me. That part was just so damn exhausted from always doing the right thing that it let go of the control. No more crying quietly. I convulsed uncontrollably. A full on snot fest of sobs belched out of me. Diola and Celine came quickly around to my side of the table and crouched by me stroking my back until my sobbing subsided a bit. Then they insisted that I not decide anything right away. I was to take a long, hot bath. While they prepared our dinner.

I gave in to their kindness. I let them run that bath. It felt so alien to me to be the one being taken care of. But I couldn't argue with them. I didn't have the strength for it. I sank back into that bath. I weirdly thought of that office team building exercise, the one where you let yourself fall into the arms of your colleague. Trusting them to catch you. My whole body let go and relaxed into that comforting warm water. Or was I collapsing back into the arms of Diola, Celine and Andy?

I lay in the steaming bath trying to think. It wasn't easy. I was stunned by their offer. Their kindness and generosity made no sense. How could they take on my sad and sorry burden? Why would they do that? Why would they choose to drag a Debbie Downer along the Camino with them? I wasn't going to be the least bit of fun. Who would want to put up with me like this? I sank right under the water and let myself float. Then it hit me. I knew that I would do the same for a friend in the same circumstances. But, not for one moment, did I think I deserved that same consideration and respect from someone else. Bath towels had been laid out for me. And in the bedroom, someone had even washed and dried my walking clothes. Boris and my things were neatly stacked on the bed. The double bed which would now be just for me. Shit, damn, I started sobbing again.

I entered the kitchen a little sheepishly, I had never, in my adult life, let myself lose control like that in front of other people. Not even my mother. I asked what I could do to help with dinner, but they told me to just sit and enjoy a glass of wine. Andy was usually head chef, but Celine had wanted to prepare a special dinner for us. And she had done a wonderful job. It was based around my favourite foods. A beautifully prepared mixed salad, scrummy tortilla and tasty little fish tapas. All beautifully laid out. What music did I want to listen to? Something uplifting. Salsa. They carried on bustling around me, laying the table, chatting easily amongst themselves. Letting me just sit there and be. Diola came and sat next to me, close enough to know she was there but not forcing me to talk. I stopped fighting the need to contribute, to be of value in some way, and sipped my wine. I let the music and their chatter flow around and seep into me. The tears had stopped, and I started to feel a warmth and contentment which was foreign to me.

Dinner over. I was not allowed to help with the cleaning up. What did I want to do next? They asked. I wanted to go dancing I said. What? That was news to me. I hadn't expected to say that. The salsa music must have had its way with me. I grabbed Celine's hand and swung her around the kitchen. We all laughed. "Let's go dancing."

Next was the matter of finding somewhere to dance. It was a Monday night. The others didn't understand what that meant. I did. In Spain, many bars and restaurants are closed on Monday nights. I knew it would be a challenge to find somewhere to dance. Diola, Celine and Andy shouted me down. "It's Spain!" they reassured me, "of course we'll find somewhere to dance." Some bars were indeed open, but not for dancing. Everyone we stopped said the same thing. "Pues, es lunes…." "Well, it's Monday…" They didn't need to say more. "I know," I said, apologetically. "My friends don't understand." We rounded a corner and a Camino miracle appeared in front of us. The door to a bar stood open. It wasn't just any bar. It was a bar with a small dance floor. Just the right size for the four of us. Hell, it even had a disco ball.

'Pues es lunes!" exclaimed the surprised barman when we asked if we could dance. His name was Alejandro. He looked us up and down, especially me, with my red rimmed eyes. And then he agreed. He started to enter into the spirit of it. Pacharans were ordered. Let the dancing begin. Alejandro obligingly played whatever track I requested. A thumbs up from me and the track played. If I made a slicing gesture across my throat, he hastily changed the song. He soon got my dance vibe. Lots of salsa. Lots of 80's disco. Nothing sad. Three dudes at the bar, in working gear, looked on in bemusement. This was obviously their local and tonight, being Monday, their night for a quiet beer. But they accepted us with good grace.

And we danced. And danced. And danced. Happily, engaged in our own little dancing bubbles. Occasionally I would grab Celine or Diola and swing them around the dance floor to the salsa beat. I wasn't brave enough to grab Andy. He did not seem like a man who would dance salsa. But he had moves. A Brit who could actually dance. Wow! And not sad dad dancing either. The music, the company and the Pacharan washed over me. Eventually, and maybe inevitably, Gloria Gaynor rang out of that little bar at full volume. She was the ace up Alejandro's sleeve. I belted out the lyrics along with Gloria. I let rip, I let it all loose, I let it all go and Alejandro, and the three dudes in the bar, and Celine, Diola and Andy, all joined me in those last three words of that chorus "I will survive!"

And in that moment, on that Monday night, on that dance floor in Gijon, I knew that I would, I would survive. And I also knew that I wasn't going anywhere. I was staying on the Camino. I bet those three dudes still talk about that Monday night. Those crazy dancing pilgrims. Pues es lunes.

Chapter 15
THE CRYING TIME

"It is such a mysterious place, the land of tears."

Antoine de Saint-Exupery

Morning came. All my bravado, of the dance floor, was gone. That fierce independent woman who had danced her socks off and belted out the words to "I Will Survive" had gone too. I just wanted to curl up in a ball, under the bedsheets, and stay there. Forever. I didn't want to do anything or go anywhere or see anyone. I didn't even want to go home. I just wanted to lie there and stop thinking, stop feeling. I wanted someone to make it all go away. If I'd had that sort of a relationship with my mum, I would have wanted her.

As I lay there with the sheets over my head I thought back over the evening before. How could I have accepted the offer of Diola, Celine and Andy to stay on the Camino with them? I was astonished that I had agreed. Last night it had seemed like the right decision. This morning it felt all wrong. I couldn't be on the receiving end of care and attention. Everything was upside down and back to front. But hiding in bed, even for one morning, was not an option for me. We were in an Airbnb. The sign on that frightening beige wall in that bland living room, 'Mi Casa es tu Casa!", "My home is your home!" was only applicable until 9am by which time we had to vacate it. Even now I could hear the sounds of backpacks being prepared, distances and destinations being discussed. I could smell the coffee brewing. That last one grabbed my attention. Coffee, everything always felt better after coffee. Maybe even this. I could give it a try.

I emerged tentatively from my bed, head a bit fuzzy, avoiding the mirror. I didn't want to see the effects of all that crying, and all that Pacharan. Stuff it! Why should I worry about what I looked like? At least I was vertical and moving. I focused on Boris. I needed to get packed up. And then it occurred to me that I should ask Pedro's opinion before I went any further. What?! Am I going crazy? Pedro's opinion? He's the reason I have to make a decision. And I was damned if I was ever going to ask him about anything ever again. Ooph. This would take some getting used to. 19 years of rubbing along together, sharing the same space, the same dreams and the same adventures was going to take some working out of my system. Focus woman, focus. One day at a time, one step at a time, right? Little ol' cliche me. I grinned, or at least I thought I was grinning. I checked it out in the mirror. It wasn't a grin; it was a grimace. Oh well, at least I was up and on my feet.

I shyly left my room. Diola, Celine and Andy were intent on packing up, checking that no lost socks were left hanging about, no walking poles lurking behind doors, no lone toothbrush in the bathroom. They greeted me warmly but didn't treat me with kid gloves. I appreciated that. I wanted normality on this morning when nothing felt normal.

Celine handed me my coffee. And then we all worked tog sure all the dishes were washed, floors swept, everything le. found it. 'Mi Casa es tu Casa!' Thank you. And we were off.

We took the bus. I no longer gave a damn about the perfect p. .n scale. Sod it. I needed to be soothed by uplifting, serene countryside. I wasn't going to walk the Camino out of Gijon with its ugly heavy industry that would reflect to me all the ugliness I felt inside. The bus dropped us off in Somewheresville, Asturias. I had no clue what the name of the village was, and I didn't care. All I knew was that it was closer to Aviles, our destination for the night, where we had booked an Airbnb house. We'd skipped quite a big climb by taking the bus, the terrain in front of me was gently undulating and undemanding of my attention. I got walking. See a yellow arrow follow a yellow arrow that was my plan.

I barrelled on, head down. I went in front of the others who, true to their word, didn't try to engage me in conversation. They waited for me to approach them if I wanted to. And I didn't. I didn't feel capable of conversation. I wanted to be alone. I tried to focus on the countryside, but my attention could only be held for so long by clouds, cows and apple trees, soooo many apple trees.

The rhythm of my steps jolted the contents of my heart upwards and outwards. Something about my constant movement, my swinging arms, all the fresh air, started to open me up despite my best attempts to cram everything back down inside. All those years maintaining a tight control on everything. My work, my weight, my diet. And my thoughts and emotions. I'd kept a vice like grip on it all. I couldn't hold it back any longer. The tsunami of tears took over. Convulsive sobs that I had not a hope in hell of stopping. The effort of holding it all in, holding it all together, was actually more painful than just letting my body have its way with me, and letting it all go.

Busy, busy, busy, I had always been busy. If I wasn't working, I was running, if I wasn't running, I was cleaning the house, if I wasn't cleaning the house, I was busy learning something new. And then when I wasn't busy, I was slumped exhausted with headphones clamped to my ears listening to podcasts, music, radio. Anything not to be alone with my thoughts and my feelings. I didn't want to know them, thank you very much. They could keep themselves to themselves. But out here on the Camino, there was no hiding from them. My thoughts and my feelings were coming for me. I might as well get it over with.

Feelings of loss, of betrayal, and grief took me over and howled their hurt. The sobbing came and went in waves as the yellow arrows made sure I stayed on the trail. Just as well, I had no clue where I was. All I knew was that I was walking through rural agricultural communities. I passed through villages that felt forgotten in time, chickens roamed free. The local communal stone wash houses called lavaderos, were still in use here. Elderly women in aprons and headscarves, with hands red raw and so gnarled that it hurt me to look at them, pounded their bed sheets into submission on the wash house stones. Their flat capped husbands, chins resting on their sticks, sat outside the village bar. Their only task staring at the passing pilgrims. I had as little interest in them as they had in me. I was just another backpacked shadow passing by on the pavement in the morning sun.

Part of me vaguely registered facts that I would have found so interesting a day ago, now they barely caught my eye. Even the signs to dolmens, ancient tombs, close to the trail which would usually have had me bounding up the track to check them out, I passed on by. I vaguely mused as to why, in Asturias, the horreos that stored grain, up high away from rats and mice, looked almost oriental with their pagoda style red tiled roofs. Did they look like that in Galicia, the next province over? I couldn't remember. I supposed I'd find out soon enough. Was I that interested, did I care? No.

I finally made it to Aviles. I met up with Celine, Diola and Andy in its colourful central plaza. Aviles was the sort of place I would usually have loved. I would have scampered through its alleyways trying to capture everything in photos. But not today. I was more interested in finding the local supermarket to get supplies for dinner and bedding down for the night.

The Airbnb experiment was working. The others had really enjoyed the comfort and privacy of the night before. They had rented us another one on the outskirts of Aviles. This time a house, old and solid, warm and welcoming with a log fire and cosy comfortable rooms. And close to my friend, the sea. We spent two days there waiting for Richard and Sarah to be drawn back into the fold. I was still reeling but my little band of friends held true to their word and left me to my own devices whilst making sure I knew they were there if I needed them.

In the evening I was ready for company. And wine. Andy set about making us a gourmet dinner, his sweet potato curry. As Andy cooked, Diola, Celine and I sat at an old worn oak table in the kitchen. We chatted and sipped our wine. Celine declared, in her outrageous French accent, "Screw 'im," meaning Pedro, "There are plenty more where 'e came from". To make her point she led the conversation to the number of partners she'd slept with. Well, she is French after all. When Andy heard the tally his kitchen knife slipped, and he nearly chopped off the end of his finger.

I was horrified at the thought of having to eventually enter the world of 21st century dating, they were filling me in on the joys of Tinder, it sounded utterly terrifying. I might prefer to hoof it back to the convent albergue in Laredo where I had played at being a hospitalera and see if they'd take me full time into their sisterhood. A life of ugly shoes and celibacy sounded far preferable to signing up for Tinder.

Dinner over, plates washed and stacked, I climbed into the old fashioned sheeted and blanketed bed, I knew that when I awoke the next morning, I'd have to go through the jangling process of remembering again what had happened. That lurch of my stomach when I slowly came to, feeling drowsily warm and safe only to be suddenly jolted into full on wakefulness by the memory that I was not safe, that the earth had shifted seismically under my feet. And that I must find the courage and energy to want to slog my way to firmer ground. I tried to remind myself that tomorrow was a fresh new start, nope, too soon for empty platitudes, nothing of substance yet to stick them to, they slithered to the floor. So once more I tried on the thought of trusting in the wisdom of the yellow arrows to guide me back to myself. One step at a time and all that. Yes, though still shallow, there was enough fertile ground for that one to take root. I sank into the slightly sagging mattress and let the creaking of the old timbers of the house, settling in for the night, lull me into a welcome temporary oblivion.

Chapter 16
THE LONG HARD LOOK

"Maybe we needed to break a little, so we could put ourselves

back together more beautifully than before.'

Leah Raeder

I knew it was time to take a long, hard look at myself. I didn't really want to, but I knew I had to. Pedro and I had been together for 19 years. His 'abandoning' me, here on the Camino, was definitely the shove I needed to face up to the truths that had been in my face for years. And so I came to realise just how true that saying is "The Camino gives you what you need, not what you want." I needed to understand what had gone wrong. This was my chance. There may never be a better time to do this. A sort of autumn cleaning of the soul.

And so, each day I forged fiercely ahead of the others. Boris was all the company I needed or could deal with. He demanded nothing of me. It was me n' Boris for life. Or, at least, for this Camino. I had had too many dysfunctional people in my life. People who had hurt me deeply. I held up all that pain to the bright daylight of the Camino to see if it was really true. I felt that I was watching a story playing out, over and over again. Each time with a different cast of characters but still all playing the same roles, in slightly different guises. Was this the Camino showing me the pattern of my life?

First was my stony-faced, shut down mother, refusing to talk with, or even acknowledge me for days on end. Then there was a moustachioed chap, who called himself my father, making sporadic visits to our home. He never came inside the house. I couldn't work out what I had done to cause that. And my stepfather, simmering with rage. We lived seemingly endless years under his reign of terror. And Pedro, whose grudges and resentments, when he thought himself to have been wronged, knew no limits. And what about this scary one - I looked just like Pedro's sister, we could have been twins. Now that in and of itself should have had me running very fast away from him. What sort of creepy was that?! That was a tough one to admit to myself.

As I walked, my juddering sobs were keeping time with my high speed staccato steps. They didn't permit deep lungfuls of air to fuel a more fluid, steady pace. My head was down, hunched over to protect myself from the inquisitive gaze of others. This further reduced my lung capacity. My laboured breathing stirred things up inside. More memories started to bubble into my consciousness. Memories I had stuffed down deep hoping to never see again. The walking was breaking them free. I wanted to speed things up, get them out and over and done with. I remembered standing with my mother on the doorstep of Janet Dominey's house. She had invited me to her birthday party. Ringing the doorbell, my nervous little face reflected in the shine of my highly polished Mary Janes, holding out a beautifully wrapped birthday present. To have the door shut in our faces. Divorcees and their daughters were not welcomed.

As the offspring of a divorcee in the '70's I had to try harder and harder to conform to whatever it took to make the grade. At my 'good school' it was crucial to keep up appearances. I remember feeling completely untethered. As if everyone around me was in on the game except for me. I was deeply envious of their sense of purpose and belonging and was desperate to get at least a taste of it. So, I doubled down on my efforts. I was always smiling and obedient. All my school reports reflected this: "Debbie is always smiling", "Debbie gives of her very best", "Debbie is highly conscientious and hardworking", "Debbie always aims to please and to help others".

So now, here I was walking alone adding a few more inches to the sea level as I traversed the beaches and villages of the beautiful Asturias coastline. I'd been so looking forward to meeting Asturias. I'd heard so much about its abundant beauty. Like a mutual friend you've known of for ages and finally have a chance to meet in person. But only a very small part of me was now registering that I was actually here and urging me to look up. I did so, and saw a hillside castle standing guard over gemstone-coloured houses dotted along the estuary below. It was like looking at a postcard, one dimensional, stripped of life. It was irrelevant to me. I was shut down to beauty. I didn't look up again. My inner antenna instinctively twitched in tune with those yellow arrows. Years of the Gucci Camino had made me sensitive to their frequency, I barely had to concentrate on them.

My gaze was focused completely within. On the landscape of my past. The truth was that for years I had been deliberately avoiding doing this. That was why I had kept myself so busy. I had to admit to myself that Pedro and I hadn't been happy for a long time. The truth was I had been staying with him out of a sense of duty. I didn't want to abandon him. What would he do here in Spain? He was here because of me. He'd always wanted to be in Argentina, but he had sacrificed being with his much loved family, having a fulfilling career, being surrounded by his friends, all to be with me. At heart he was a very compassionate and caring person. I had had many a conversation with him about the silent treatment he gave me. I always ended up feeling sorry for him for acting in this way. I thought it must come from a deep source of pain within him.

A conversation with his mother came back to me. She was an incredibly kind and compassionate woman, always positive and smiling. I asked her about Pedro's moodiness and how he would often refuse to acknowledge my existence. She suddenly turned harsh, almost accusatory and said words to the effect of: 'Well you chose to be with him, you've made your bed now you have to lie in it'. And his sister added "You can't give him back now. You've taken him on. He's yours. There's no returning him". Ugh, where did this leave me now? I took a deep breath and reminded myself that all was OK. I'd find the right answer. The Camino was holding me in its embrace. I would get through this.

The weather had turned wet and windy. So, I stopped for a coffee on the vine covered terrace of a local bar. It served as the focal point of the tiny community I was passing through. Selling essential groceries, stamps, cigarettes, everything needed to keep life ticking over as it had been for decades. A huge mastiff hound that I could have ridden the Camino on, barely stirred as I stepped over him. His massive head lifted a fraction from the stone floor, nothing of interest here, just another sad soul seeking warmth and comfort. On the worn metal tables, it was no longer possible to make out the brand of beer they had originally been advertising, the message buried under decades of wear, innumerable cups of coffee, wine or beer served to the passing pilgrim.

An elderly woman in a creased but clean blue tabard placed a steaming bowl of cafe con leche on the table in front of me. She retreated behind the old stable door without a word, just a slight nod of her head. I noticed that she was wearing wooden clogs. Rough hewn madreñas, hollowed out of birch wood with four small stilts on each corner to keep the wearer's feet up and out of the mud. I'd seen them used as flowerpots, decorative mementos of a bygone era. Who would choose to put those instruments of torture on their feet nowadays? Only someone who was firmly rooted in their traditional way of life, I thought. I was envious of her grounded existence. She knew who she was and where she belonged, she had a solid identity. She didn't need to walk 500 miles to come back to herself. She was home. Unlike me. I was the modern pilgrim, in my high-tech hiking shoes, feeling untethered as I walked on the shifting sands of my memories, trying to find myself.

I sat and nursed my coffee letting the soothing sounds of the local news on the telly drift out to me along with the acrid smoke of the black Ducados tobacco. Smoking might have been banned in bars since 2011 in Spain, but here, where I was sitting, stood outside of time and convention. They lived in a rhythm of their own. It made me feel like the company of my Camino family. I hoped one of them would catch up with me and stop here.

Diola arrived. She was the perfect salve for my raw, ragged hurt. She listened. Most people never truly listen as they are already forming their responses and judgments before you've even finished talking. Not Diola. She let me see that I had enough strength and knowing within me. She let me work out my own answers. She was an intensely private person, but she shared some of her story with me. She'd just split up with her long term boyfriend and was herself getting over the hurt of it all and working out what to do next. I felt honoured. I knew she wouldn't open up to just anyone. It was inspiring to see just how capable and independent she was. It made me feel that I could possibly have some of that strength within me too.

By the time I had finished walking for the day I felt wrung out, but a little lighter. I was ready for, and welcomed the easy, relaxed company of my Camino family again. I don't remember what was said during those evening conversations, the content of which was unimportant, what I do remember is the sense of camaraderie and so much bloody fun and laughter. Sarah was a great cook as was Andy and they made some lovely meals followed, of course, by our favourite, Pacharan. And then loads more laughter. In fact, Sarah was always laughing or about to laugh. She was easy, good company with her no nonsense, up and at 'em approach to life. No warm and fuzzy, no going deep. She was a practical woman. Her feet were firmly planted on the ground. And that was a relief to me. Her Canadian husband, Richard was quiet, unassuming and kind, and easy to be with. Sarah was partly British, although having lived her life in Canada she really appreciated reconnecting with the wicked sense of British humour that Andy regaled us with in spades. As did I. I absolutely loved living in Spain but there is nothing like the British sense of humour. I think you must be born with one to survive the UK weather and general air of gloominess that prevails there.

Talking of Andy, well he was the biggest surprise of the lot. He wasn't only bloody funny; he was also extremely wise. That court jester persona housed a caring and empathetic soul. For good reason he had been given custody of his four small children at a time that most courts would automatically grant custody to the mother. And I admired his resolve and commitment at having brought them up, even home schooling them from a very young age. He never said what he thought I wanted to hear. He was honest when I asked his advice. He didn't sugar-coat things. And after dispensing his pearls of wisdom he would make some amusing quip that made me laugh through my tears, laughing at myself, laughing at ALL of it.

At this time, we were subbing Celine as she was low on funds. But even with that when it was her turn to take the couch or the bunk bed, she would still argue the point. "Mais pour quoi?" "But why me?" She would protest. She fully expected the universe to provide for her. And so, it did. She wanted me to slow down and commune with nature as she did. She said it would be good for me. She loved to hug trees, especially great big old oak trees. I don't think I had ever actually met anyone that genuinely hugged trees before. I had always thought it was an exaggerated depiction of someone with 'hippy' tendencies. But she actually did hug them and hang out with them. She said she threw her arms around them as far as she could reach and hugged. Then, she said she sat in their comforting shade. Often. And she didn't give a flying fig who saw her or what they thought. I wasn't going to do anything like that. I couldn't chance it. What if someone saw me do it? Too risky! I was way too self-conscious. Celine didn't care what other people thought of her. I did care. And I was starting to realise that in that 'care' I was caring about all the wrong things.

Chapter 17
GOING FOR GOLD

"You are an alchemist, make gold of that."

William Shakespeare

Reeling from a recent separation? Head straight to the Camino. All you need is a decent pair of broken in walking shoes, one set of walking clothes, two sets of undies, a sleeping bag and a rain poncho, anything that you're tempted to take based on the fear of needing it, ruthlessly ignore. If it turns out that you did need it, you won't care. The Camino gives you everything you need.

Now I was noticing something on the Camino I hadn't noticed before. Other lone pilgrims walking, head down, inwardly focused just like me. Both men and women, but the majority women. We were vaguely aware of each other's presence. We knew not to 'Buen Camino' one another. We formed a sub-category of pilgrims. I felt we should have our own secret handshake. A tribe of wandering, lost souls looking for pieces of ourselves along the way. Maybe that's why we walked with our heads bowed. Unlike me, they often walked at a snail's pace, even stopping, evidently in deep inner contemplation. That wasn't my way. It felt as if the faster I moved the more that onward motion powered my going within. I wasn't running away from myself but into myself.

It felt comforting to know it wasn't just me on this lone sob-fest while all the other pilgrims were having one long party to which I wasn't invited. In fact, if crying whilst walking was an Olympic sport, let's say "power-crying", I was going for gold. Sometimes my crying was uncontrollable. I would have to give in to it and stop, doubled over ,because I literally couldn't breathe. It occurred to me that the name given to the 'hospitaleros' in the albergues, those dedicated people looking out for the pilgrims' needs, was quite fitting. They were given that name because the albergues were originally hospitals for sick and wounded pilgrims needing to rest and recover from their physical ailments. A lot of us pilgrims were hurting, but like me, it was not a physical pain we were trying to heal.

I started to observe my weeping walker tribe as I overtook them on the trail, or while I was having my coffee fix at midday, or when I was taking a quick breather. Wondering what their story was. Wondering what they were walking to overcome. Wondering what drama was being played out in their world. I was sure their stories held some common threads with mine. The 'if onlys', the 'what was I thinking', the 'where did I go wrongs'.

Each of us, our own individual planet of pain, spinning along the path. Each of us a separate story, divided into chapters that we were leafing through hoping to come up with a different and better ending. There were those of us that walked to grieve the loss of a loved one, a spouse, a parent, or surely the ultimate anguish, a child. Those who had just received 'the call' from the doctor who had given them the dreaded diagnosis, the snuffing out of that final flicker of hope. And they had come to the Camino knowing that miracles have happened here.

Pilgrims with terminal illnesses have had remissions after walking the Camino.

Then there were those who walked to be forgiven for a sin they themselves could barely believe they had committed. Something had snapped within them, one split second loss of control giving into the impulse they would barely even admit to having within them, let alone carry it out. A plot twist so unexpected you would scoff at the author for over-stretching your imagination. None a straightforward formulaic story arc of generic grief. Each of us a complicated structure of plots and sub-plots.

When I was younger, I tried the conventional religious route, but it didn't inspire me. I couldn't find within the Church what I was searching for. I wanted to. I would have dearly loved to have found solace there, to have a prescribed set of rules to follow. But then here I was, a pilgrim along with thousands of other pilgrims on one of the holiest pilgrimage routes in Europe, seeking relief from my inner turmoil. What was the healing power of the Camino? Was it simply the effects of the walking and oxygen, all those endorphins charging around my systems? Or was there more? Was there a higher power involved?

To me that power felt 'spiritual' in nature, whatever the hell that meant. Some described the Camino as a crucible in which the ingredients of pain and suffering could be alchemised, and the pilgrim would be born anew. Could I be born anew? I wasn't sure that was possible. I would keep walking and find out. Maybe the intentions of those millions of people who had gone before me, had imbued the earth over which I tromped with an energy that would worm its way up into my body.

Starting at my feet, wriggling its way up and into my heart and mind. Whatever it was, something was going on, but I let go of the need to name and categorise it. I was here to relinquish control. Control, I realised, was only an illusion. My seemingly unscalable defences that had felt safe and solid, like an impenetrable armour, had been torn down.

I wasn't unique even though what I was going through was deeply personal and hugely important to me. I was just one of millions of women and men going through a mid-life separation. I certainly couldn't have planned a better place for it to happen. This was the one place perhaps in the world where we could have an abundance of time and space for reflection. Hours of solitude in which to contemplate, evaluate and face up to the truths that had been in our faces for years but which some of us had determinedly dodged. Thank God I'd decided to stay here. It almost felt as if this was actually meant to have happened. That it had been the perfect plan for me all along. To brutally yank me out of that deep pit of denial. And give into the healing power of the Camino. Not the plan that I'd made for myself and thought that I'd wanted. But the one that I needed. The Camino knew what it was doing. I was glad that someone did. It meant that I didn't need to for once. I could let go for the first time and give in to what it needed to teach me. Here there were no more excuses, there was nowhere to go other than westwards and within. So, on I strode.

Chapter 18
THE PEOPLE PLEASER

"The problem is, when you work so hard

to get everyone to like you,

you very often end up

not liking yourself so much."

Reshma Saujani

Every morning now, I was spending less time on the crying Camino, the tears were slowly drying up. We were now in a proper Airbnb groove, the next one we had chosen was in the town of Muros de Nalon. When we got to the address, the Airbnb simply did not exist. I called the listed phone number, but no one answered. There was nothing I could do. We walked back to the town square and found somewhere we could take off our backpacks, rest our feet, have a drink and come up with a new plan for the night.

After half an hour an irate woman called on my phone asking where on earth we were. I told her what had happened, that we had tried to find her Airbnb but the address on the website was wrong. An old, very familiar anxiety came over me. I felt a desperate desire to placate her. And I felt guilty for keeping her waiting. She shared her location with me via WhatsApp and I said I would meet her there immediately. I grabbed my things to leg it there as fast as possible.

A hand, gently but firmly, pushed me back down into my seat. "Take your time, finish your drink," Andy instructed. "She is the one at fault. She should be apologising to you for not providing the correct address. You should not be apologising to her for her mistake. She can wait until you are ready". It was agony for me to sit back down. Diola, Celine, Sarah, Richard and Andy watched me like hawks. They understood very little Spanish, but my body language and my tone must have let them in on the phone conversation. I had to force myself not to gulp down my drink and scarper.

Richard was dispatched to accompany me to meet the lady and collect the keys. He was under strict instructions, "Don't let her apologise." He watched my every move. And my every word. It was excruciating. I was desperate to say, 'Lo siento', 'I'm sorry'. I was caught between two enormous impulses; one was to placate the Airbnb owner and the other to please my Camino family.

The next morning, over my coffee, I pondered my intense reaction to the irate lady and her Airbnb. When Diola joined me, I asked her if she thought that maybe I might be one of those sad people who tried really hard to please other people. She threw her hands up in the air and said "D'ya think?!!" In such a way as to leave me in no doubt that it was indeed true and blindingly obvious to everyone. Except me.

As we were making our way out of Muros de Nalon, a car stopped and a friendly, beaming local chap suggested that we take a deviation away from the Camino down to the beautiful beach of Playa del Aguilar. He enthused that it was the most exquisite beach we would ever see. We would normally resist adding more milage to our day but today we were only walking 15 kms to Soto de Luina. We all agreed it would indeed be a shame to deprive ourselves of this opportunity.

I, once again went ahead of the others, barrelling down the quiet rural roads towards the beach and my friend the ocean. I was intent on puzzling out this idea that I might be a people pleaser. As I walked, I started to understand it better. Diola and the others had seen me with Pedro, twisting myself inside out in my attempt to please and placate him. That certainly would make them think that I was a people pleaser.

But surely my people pleasing tendencies didn't hold sway in all my decisions? What about now heading to Playa del Aguilar, was it just to please that proud local man? Yes, it was. I had to admit that to myself. And I had to admit I was relieved we were only walking 15 kms today so there was no argument from the others against going down to the beach. I didn't want to disappoint that man and I don't like to disappoint people generally. "Nothing wrong with that, right?" I thought. "I always do what is asked of me and give of it my best." It was quite a steep descent down to 'the most beautiful beach in Asturias' and as I carefully placed my feet, it occurred to me that I wanted to please people because I didn't want them to be disappointed in me. I didn't want them to say that I wasn't good enough. That stopped me. "That's not good," I thought as I continued down and around the last bend.

Playa del Aguilar now revealed itself in all its glory. And yes, it was very beautiful. A vast sweep of fine golden sand, overlooked by wooded clifftops. But that described dozens of similar beaches we had marched over, around and above over the last few weeks. So beautiful is the Camino del Norte. The others caught up with me and having taken this long, sharp downhill detour to marvel at the beach, we now had the corresponding steep climb back up to the Camino. I was so engrossed in my thoughts it made little difference to me what terrain my feet were walking over. Not sure the others felt the same way.

I felt almost removed from my physical body, so deep was I in contemplation as I made the steep ascent. I wondered if, even now, I was still navigating my life by the same tools as I had as that child trying so desperately to please her father. I had certainly had many difficult and demanding people in my life. Pedro was definitely a prime example. When one of his gloomy moods descended and he retreated into himself, barely acknowledging my existence, I was left squirming in discomfort, looking for ways to put things right, to claw my way back into his affection or at least his approval. I tried endlessly to wave my magic wand to make him happy.

I continued climbing. And as I did, I shone my headlamp within. And I shone it on a small child who had felt abandoned by a father who had fled the family to form another. Soon after I was born. He had run off with a woman with whom he had a daughter born at roughly the same time as me. I was the faulty goods he had exchanged. She was the upgraded, more acceptable, more lovable version. Still, he returned on various occasions to test drive me. Always at lunch in stiffly starched restaurants, where children were barely tolerated. Despite my attempts to mind my p's and q's and be the sort of child who earned her entrance ticket into his high society, I was always found wanting, like the faulty goods I was. Returned and deposited on my mother's doorstep.

In my professional life, too. I was known as the go to person for dealing with difficult clients. When the shit hit the fan, I was the one to go in and scoop up the poop. Lost passports, missed trains and planes, broken down buses, overbooked hotels, sick students, even the death of clients. I defused situations fraught with stress. Always I could be depended on to find a way to appease and please. This was my 'skill', my badge of honour. I could make the most difficult of clients happy. Twisting myself into uncomfortable contortions in an attempt to be what others needed me to be. I remember a colleague telling me that my job would consist of "pissing off the smallest amount of people possible" which implied that someone was still going to be bloody pissed off. Which to me was excruciating. I lived in a permanent state of anxiety.

I definitely put my needs and wants last if I put them anywhere at all, if I was even aware of having needs. On a sliding scale from one to ten I was so far to the left as to not even register on the scale. I would give myself maybe a minus five. Sod it. I had obviously spent my whole life people pleasing, that was going to have to change. I would have to be as brave and bold as I knew how. I would have to recalibrate and find a new place of balance within me where I wasn't bloody apologising for my very existence.

As I walked, I thought about Diola and Celine. They weren't people pleasers like me. Diola clearly and confidently expressed her wants and needs. She did this whilst also being very sensitive to the wants and needs of others. Celine, on the other hand, was very firm that her wants and needs came first. She was the opposite pole to me and yet she was still a genuinely caring, well-meaning and kind person. I could now see that my total self-effacement was unnecessary and had been deeply damaging. I had these two wonderful women to help me overcome this strange, debilitating pattern of behaviour. Like Goldilocks, I would have to find the chair, the bed, the bowl, the place that felt just right for me. I would have to let these two remarkable women help me do that.

As I approached our stopping point, Soto De Luina, the weather was changing fast. The sky was darkening and yet it was only early afternoon. No worries, we'd soon be tucked up in a cosy albergue. Except that all the pilgrims who hadn't taken that detour down to the 'most beautiful beach in Asturias' had got here first. And the municipal albergue and the other reasonably priced hotel option in town were already full up. No Airbnb options to be had either. Bugger. We would have to continue on to the next town, Ballota. I was really looking forward to walking that next stretch. I had heard that it was lovely, and only about another 11 kms on. I wanted to walk. I wasn't going to let a few drops of pending rain stop me. The others weren't keen on walking given the weather. But they were, by now, familiar with my need to walk on by myself and didn't try to dissuade me.

There was a tiny train station in Soto de Luina. They checked to see if they could hop a train to Ballota and meet up with me there. Except that Celine was missing in action. She still hadn't caught up with us. Doubtless she had her arms wrapped around a tree trunk somewhere along the trail. A WhatsApp message pinged in to confirm this. She wouldn't make it in time for the last train. We sat a little dejected in a local bar to consider our options. I called an albergue in Ballota to at least secure beds for us for the night. We sent Richard on ahead, he could very easily outride the bad weather. By the time Celine had finished communing with the trees and found us, Diola, Andy, Sarah and she had decided to grab a taxi. I put Boris in with them and prepared to hoof it. The driver stashed the packs and invited me to sit up front with him. When I told him that I was walking on, he physically grabbed me by the shoulders and turned me in the direction of the ominously black oncoming storm clouds, 'Are you completely insane?' would be the polite version of what he said. I hated to admit it, but I knew that he was completely right. Just as the first rumbles of thunder started to reverberate around the hills and the rain started to lash down, I jumped in. Humbled, I sat meekly in the front seat of the taxi and realised what a complete arse I could have made of myself if I had tried to make it to Ballota in those conditions.

The hostal in Ballota was basic but warm and dry. I love these really local establishments that also serve as albergues. The albergue was sometimes something of an afterthought but that was just fine with me. We were the only pilgrims there. We had the dormitory, and the hot water, to ourselves. We got an upfront and personal glimpse into the lives of the villagers. The bar was humming with locals discussing the storm that raged outside. We were wrapped in the warm fug of cigarette smoke. Who was going to be enforcing EU legislation out here? In the huge fireplace smoke was belching out as the flames started to nibble away at logs the size of small cars. Farm workers in overalls mingled with the street sweepers, even the postman perched at the bar, no letter, however urgent, could trump the need for shelter from the storm. As opposed to city life, here the villagers doffed their cap in deference to nature's far superior rank. There was an air of bunking off school, of an unexpected half day holiday.

Card decks were shuffled. Carajillos - coffee with large doses of brandy were ordered. We commandeered the abandoned football table and started an international tournament. The small red and white figures whirled wildly as Canada competed fiercely with England and France and Germany had a nail-biting penalty shoot out.

Chapter 19

LOVELY LUARCA

"You know, one day you look at the person and you see

something more than you did the night before.

Like a switch had been flicked somewhere.

And the person who was just a friend is…suddenly the only person

You can ever imagine yourself with."

Gillian Anderson

O ur next port of call was Luarca. And port indeed it was, a gorgeous little fishing village that I had heard a lot about and was looking forward to getting to know.

We had all regrouped in a cafe about 8 kms before Luarca. All except Andy. No one had seen him for some time. But we had all witnessed his trying to gamely pretend that he wasn't struggling. We weren't in any particular hurry, so I left Boris with them and jogged back along the Camino. After a kilometre or so I saw his Tilley hat approaching. Head down it bobbed slowly and painfully towards me. When he finally looked up, I was almost upon him. He was shocked to see me and not altogether pleased that I had seen his ungainly progress. I made light of my being there and said I had just fancied a bit of a jog. He was most uncharacteristically subdued. I could see that he was hurting like hell. Knowing that he would never hand over his backpack willingly, I suggested he take it off and rest for a bit. As it hit the ground I whipped it away from him. 'C'mon the others are waiting for us with a coffee to revive you', I said. He was mortified to have me carry his pack. I moved away fast. He would have to catch me to get it off me. He made it to the cafe. But only just. Being looked after was evidently a role he was not comfortable with. I could empathise with that and tried to downplay it.

I checked with the barman about local buses. There wasn't one due for hours and the only taxi was out and wouldn't be back any time soon. Andy would have to hitch hike. I thought about going with him but two self-conscious Brits feeling a bit awkward about hitching a ride didn't sound a like a winning solution. Celine was our secret weapon. I knew she would have no issue with thumbing a ride and would easily get a car to stop. I could just imagine her sticking her thumb out, then Andy limping out of the shadows to jump into the car too. Her magic worked. She managed to get them a ride all the way to the Airbnb flat we were renting. The driver spoke only Spanish, Andy spoke only English and Celine spoke only a tiny bit of Spanish. But still they managed to communicate. Celine's effortless spontaneous charm and beauty once again made others keen to please her.

She sent us a Whats App message when Andy and she arrived in Luarca. She had meant to write 'fellow pilgrims' but her phone autocorrected it into 'fellow pigeons' which seemed sort of apt on two fronts. It wouldn't be unkind to say that she spoke a sort of pidgin

English. Her Camino was turning, amongst other things, into a crash course in English. Of which she spoke some, and was improving by the day. The fact that she didn't have the inhibitions of so many of us when speaking a language in which she was much less than fluent helped a lot. And of course, that beautiful French accent made everything sound all the more charming in and of itself. And we were indeed pigeons. Homing pigeons! Sometimes we would be out flying solo during the day, but we all came together again to roost in the evening. So, from then on, we called ourselves pigeons.

Walking into Luarca I had to admit to feeling very sad. This was a place that Pedro and I had been looking forward to visiting for a long time. When we were on the Gucci Camino, having finished with one group in Santiago and on our way back to Bilbao to pick up our next group, we would overnight in a grotty hostel on the motorway. The address of which said Luarca, but it was a truck stop that could have been anywhere in the world. The next day, as we prepared to leave, we would catch whiffs of sea air drifting in on the early morning breeze. And once en route, from the motorway we would turn and look longingly at the vignette of the village, at its picture-perfect little bay, complete with brightly coloured bobbing boats. So near and yet so far. One day, we always said, we would get to stay there. So that day was finally here but Pedro wasn't, and it did actually feel very, very odd.

I offered to accompany Andy to the clinic to translate for him. It was a Sunday. In Spain no one likes to work on a Sunday. And worse still, it was Sunday afternoon. The doctor on duty was not impressed when we woke him up from his siesta. He exacted his revenge by thrusting his hand unceremoniously down Andy's trousers much to Andy's dismay. I averted my gaze but not before I'd giggled at Andy's shocked expression. He looked exactly like the stunned emoji. The good doctor prescribed two days' rest after which Andy would be fine to continue his Camino.

We had scored ourselves a great Airbnb with huge picture windows opening out over the harbour. We held a family conference and told Andy that we would all like to stay on in Luarca for an extra day as it was such a beautiful place. If that was OK with him. He, of course, saw through this and said that he didn't expect us to wait around for him, but we ignored him, and happily made arrangements to thoroughly enjoy this charming little spot. Sarah and Richard, however, were going to head off on their bikes one day sooner than us. They were not people to slow down. They were supremely fit even though they were of an age when most people were hanging up their running or working shoes and reaching for their slippers. I don't think Richard was the sort of guy who could rest for longer than one day, it wasn't in his genetic make-up. He was always enthusiastically searching out and embracing new challenges. We knew we would catch up with them again shortly. They could run (or cycle) but they couldn't hide from us.

At the end of that first day, we gathered together and sat on the bench outside the house, listening to music and enjoying the last of the day's sunshine. Andy offered to make us another of his, by now famous, sweet potato curries. He had already been out and bought the ingredients. We didn't need asking twice and made our way down the stairs into the kitchen. Sarah put on some soft music. Celine decorated the table with candles and a jar of wildflowers. I uncorked the wine. The kitchen was in the basement of the house. Snug and cosy. Boat themed blue and white ceramic tiles reflected in the glow of the candlelight. A basket of logs for the old-fashioned pot belly stove nestled in the corner. My sadness at being here without Pedro was totally gone. I was completely content, in this moment, with my Camino family. I hovered above the scene for a bit and took it in. Sometimes I find I can look back nostalgically at a particular moment in time and wish I had known how special it was whilst I was actually living it. This was not such a moment. I was living it, and full appreciating every second as it was happening. I was keenly aware that it was a special time, a time that I would never forget.

Dishwasher stacked, drowsy with wine and the delicious meal, Sarah, Richard, Celine and Diola drifted off to bed. Andy and I were about to follow in their wake, just lingering over the last drops of wine in our glasses. Leaving us at a candlelit table for two. Soft music and flowers adding extra ambience. The easy warm companionship of a few seconds ago shifted into a slightly awkward awareness of this parody of a romantic moment. I was suddenly ridiculously aware of our hands resting close together on the tabletop. Absurdly, I felt myself sucked into the role of woman at candlelit dinner for two. Obviously just a delusional effect of the warmth and the wine. But the hilarious bald Brit I had been walking with for days, with whom I'd felt completely relaxed, to whom I had revealed myself warts and all, had left the table. In his place was sitting a kind, warm, gentle, lovely man with whom I felt suddenly and inexplicably shy and awkward. What the hell?! I turned away from him for a moment but when I looked back this imposter was still there. I yawned unconvincingly, shot up from my chair, turned off the music and switched on the overhead light. I started bustling around the kitchen chucking the remaining wine down the sink and clattering the glasses into the dishwasher. When I turned back Andy had gone. Not just the character who had suddenly replaced the funny bald chap I had been walking with. The real Andy had left the kitchen too. Thank God. What the f. was that about?!

I decided it was definitely the stupid candles. What was I thinking? That I was in some sort of idiotic rom com? It was just good old Andy for God's sake. I was utterly absurd to make anything of this. Good God I'd literally been separated from my husband for all of six days! Haha God, just imagine leaping straight into something with a virtual stranger, just when I was celebrating getting to know and like myself for the first bloody time ever. What a moronic move that would be. I slammed shut the kitchen door on both the room and my still whirling thoughts and emotions.

The next day I put on my running shoes. Running is how I love to explore a place and its surroundings. OK, running is also one of my go-to avoidance strategies. I was running away from Andy. Running away from all those unwanted thoughts and feelings of that Sunday night. I ran. This imposter masquerading as Andy, was making me feel bloody preposterous sensations. I already had far more than enough on my plate to deal with in getting to know myself and what I wanted next from life. I most certainly didn't need the added complication of some absurd Camino crush.

The best spot from which to take in all of Luarca was the cemetery at the top of the village. Talk about a tomb with a view. A panoramic postcard with that colourful tug boated harbour, the Bay of Biscay beyond and yet another classic, Camino del Norte, pepper pot lighthouse. I was happy just sitting and contemplating that vista. For the first time in many, many years it was just me. And I loved that. I didn't need to consult with anyone but myself. I could feel things starting to whir and click within me. New sensations starting to bubble their way up from within. Those feelings had been long suppressed by my well-rehearsed regime of being frantically busy and stressed. Right now, I had no pressing deadlines to meet, no urgent calls to take, no emergency situations to fly to. I had no excuses. The Camino was in charge and was raising the temperature. I just had to hold on and go with it.

Chapter 20

ARMED AND ANGRY

"Anger is like flowing water;

there is nothing wrong with it if you let it flow."

C. Joybell C.

In a day or so the yellow arrows would be turning me inland away from the coast. So, the next morning, even though I really, really hated getting sand in my shoes, I stopped and went down to thank the sea in person, to spend a while with it. It was the least I could do. It had been a source of such comfort to me with its constant, soothing presence. It had graciously accepted my tears, tossing me a life jacket when I needed it. Providing me with a safe place to dump all that pain overboard so that I didn't need to fear drowning in my own seemingly never ending ocean of grief.

I stepped down into a small, compact horseshoe shaped bay. A little flying carpet of soft sand fitted snugly within the steep cliff walls. I passed a rowing boat with its oars placed neatly together like hands folded in prayer. I ran my hands over the rock faces, admiring the many layers of colour that formed them. I followed the line of the rock face which took me under an overhang obscuring tunnels and caves hidden deep within those rocks. They had doubtless born witness to countless mysteries and secrets. I said my goodbyes and headed back up to the track to follow the yellow arrows to Ribadeo, our next stop.

I wasn't an angry person, I thought as I emptied the sand out of my walking shoes. I knew for sure that I wasn't. I had awarded myself my personal badge of honour for not being an angry person. If I had allowed myself to be an angry person, I wouldn't have been the saint in all my relationships. And my friends wouldn't have been able to marvel at such saintly selflessness. At least I thought that was what they did. I wasn't sure anymore. But, even so, as I got motoring in the direction of Ribadeo, something strange was happening deep within me. I became aware of foreign little creatures within clamouring for my attention. What were they? I sprang the cage door and let them loose to see. They were angry little creatures.

They riled me up. I couldn't remember ever feeling like this before. I was angry. I was thundering along the Camino now. I was causing shock waves that would have registered from Santiago de Compostela all the way along the Camino del Norte back to Irun. No more tears, no more sorrow and sadness over my failed marriage. I was truly angry about it. I flailed my way through fields, railing against Pedro. How dare he treat me like this. I was angry with him for his cowardice, the way he had left me after 19 years. I was angry with him for the silent treatment he always gave me so he could get his own way. And most of all I was angry with his entitled laziness, his unwillingness to take a job, any job, to help us out. And then I got angry with every other dysfunctional person that had played a part in my life. And it felt bloody good.

I was now the mad muttering woman on the Camino. A surly scowl replacing my tear stained face. Locals averted their gaze when I passed through villages. Some older women, I noticed, seemed to hold my challenging stare with a knowing gaze. Angry woman on the Camino. They had seen this before. I thrashed my walking poles as I stomped along the path. "Buen Camino" be damned. I was done with being a good A+pilgrim. Heaven help any unsuspecting pilgrim that didn't move over fast enough on those narrow rural pathways. Get out of my way before I impale you on my walking poles.

As I took a breather, approaching the long bridge into Ribadeo, I made a decision. I was not going to edit myself anymore. I was going to express all that I was feeling and thinking. OK I knew that wouldn't make me pleasant company. Sod it. I had spent my whole life turning myself inside out just to be pleasant company. No more report cards that said, "Debbie always aims to please and to help others". No more minding my p's and q's to gain someone's affection. I was going to recalibrate myself. I would have to dig deep and find my self-respect. Obviously, it was extremely precarious. Just a wafer thin base, plywood at best. I needed to build it into a solid, substantial platform of steel. This must be why I was here on the Camino, this must be why this configuration of people, places and events had lined up, so that I would finally, with this hammer blow from Pedro, understand that the love, respect, approval and appreciation that I had been looking for from others could never, ever come if I didn't first give it to myself.

It got me sooo angry to think about myself and my part in all of this. It made me fairly squirm. It was only now that I realised that I had been a doormat. I had imprisoned myself. No one had done it to me. I had done it all to myself. So stupid of me. Ugh! I had been having a full-on pity party. Over the years I had bleated my sad story to all my friends. And my friends had tut-tutted along in sympathy. At the time it had felt soothing but now I knew it was a choice that I had made that rendered me powerless, stuck and trapped. I had avoided looking at the state of my marriage. I had kept myself running at full tilt. Always working. Telling myself I had no choice because I was providing for both of us. Never a single word from me reproaching Pedro for not doing his fair share. I was the saint bringing home the bacon. Too busy to look at what was going on with Pedro and me. Ha! I had made very bloody sure of that.

In that crazy moment it occurred to me for the first time ever that I was perfectly safe. And that it was OK for me to take responsibility for all that had happened to me. Everything that had happened had brought me to this moment, here on the Camino. And that included anything that I might have labelled as bad or unjust. As I stood staring at my next yellow arrow leading me on to the bridge into Ribadeo I knew I had the power within me to step out of my endless story loop of pleasing and appeasing. I had never questioned the way the story was going. But now, thanks to that phone call from Pedro I was tearing that script up.

I thought about forgiving all those dysfunctional people in my life, but I realised that I had already done it. I had walked all the anger and frustration out of me. There was nothing to forgive. I was free. It was a slightly giddying but exciting prospect. At last, I could unzip my straight jacket of strictly controlled thoughts and beliefs. My life wasn't beige like that living room in that house back in Gijon. There was a whole palette of wonderful colours for me to play with in my future.

Fittingly, as I crossed over the seemingly endless 'Puente de los Santos', 'Bridge of the Saints', into Ribadeo and Galicia, I let my self imposed mantel of martyrdom slip from my shoulders to the ground, to be trampled into oblivion by all those who would follow in my footsteps.

As I walked into the village square, I spotted a plaque naming the square the 8th of March. My birthday. And International Women's Day. Bloody brilliant. I had to have a photo with this. I spotted a fast-retreating Tilley hat. It was Andy trying to slope past me. I demanded that he come back and take my photo. Andy of course agreed. He suggested that I might want to smile. I suggested that he might want to shove one of his walking poles where the sun don't shine. Poor chap, what was it he'd done wrong again? Oh yes, I remembered. I was falling in love with him.

Chapter 21
THE SONGS OF GALICIA

"Music acts like a key,

to which the most tightly closed heart opens."

Maria von Trapp

The aroma of freshly brewed coffee gradually filtered through my dreams, and I drowsily stirred in my bed, heavy limbed and contented. Letting one of my very favourite smells slowly stir me into wakefulness. Lovely, someone had already been up and prepared the coffee. As I gradually started to come around, I realised that the smell was so strong, it seemed as if that coffee was right next to me. I blearily urged my eyes to open just a slit and saw a steaming mug sitting next to me on the bedside table. Huh? Then a hand gently touched my shoulder. 'Are you awake?' Said a disembodied voice.

Holy shit.

I recognised that voice. And I remembered that I hadn't slept alone. Gradually it came back to me. I had stopped feeling angry the previous evening. I had stopped feeling sad and lonely and afraid and ashamed and all the other rollercoaster emotions I had been experiencing. I simply felt uncomplicated happiness. Not needing anything or anyone else. Happy just to be me, exactly as I was and where I was.

Let's go back a step.

After Andy took my photo on the 8th of March square in Ribadeo I collected the house keys for our Airbnb. I then went to the local supermarket to buy everyone's favourite things for a pre-dinner tapas. Spicy peppers for Diola. Serrano ham for Andy. Soft Asturian cheese for Celine. As well as favourite beers and delicious local white wine. (Sarah and Richard were still a day ahead of us). I got in croissants for everyone (but me) to have in the morning. It was my little thank you for their tolerance and acceptance of me. They had been true to their word taking and accepting me just as I was. And I knew I hadn't been easy company. I didn't need to make a song and dance of it. They could see that it was now safe to be with me and we settled back into our relaxed familiar routine. Diola taking Andy's phone to connect him to the wifi. He was dyslexic and found the endless chain of letters and numbers a pain to deal with. Celine bursting spontaneously into song as she got ready to go out. Andy getting the wood in for the fire. We knew each other's ways. Like the family that we were.

Sarah and Richard had given us a recommendation for dinner that night. The restaurant was just as warm and welcoming as Sarah and Richard had described it. Wooden barrels lined the walls, low lighting, rough-hewn wooden tables, a sawdust floor, paper tablecloths. Low key and homely. Cider was expertly poured in a honey coloured arc, but without any pomp and circumstance. Delicious, unpretentious home cooked fare was placed unceremoniously on the table. Huge tortillas overhung the edges of the plates, squidgy and liquid in the centre just as I loved it. Prawns floated in a sea of hot oil and garlic. Diola's favourite, Padron peppers, crispy and just that touch burnt, giving them all the more flavour. Locals and pilgrims, all were welcomed equally.

At the table next to ours sat a circle of women of all ages. Young women with babies on their laps, little girls with old fashioned ribbons in their hair ran in airplane circles around them, middle aged women lipsticked and smartly attired, carefully coiffed, fur coated grandmothers. I asked them if they were celebrating a special occasion. They told me that it was the annual outing of the regional women's choir. Later they set to singing their local ballads which had been passed down to them through the generations. Soulfully and tunefully reaching within us all to a place that recognised the sentiments if not the words. Pilgrims were respectfully quiet and attentive. All deeply moved. Aware that we were blessed to be included in this intimate moment of local life that they generously shared with us. No sign up saying a private party was going on. Strangers and lifelong friends and family were all included. It was a special moment for each of us. I saw even tough old Andy getting a little misty eyed.

And then we all walked home tired and happy, ready to settle down for the night and contemplate another glorious day on the Camino. It was my turn to take the couch. It was Andy's turn to get the best room. Always the gentleman, he was ready to take the couch, but we all insisted that he must take his turn too. I went to check out his sumptuous upstairs 'suite'. It was palatial, huge luxurious double bed and en-suite bathroom. I sat on the edge of the bed, and we chatted about how special the evening had been. Then that thing that had happened in the kitchen in Luarca happened again. Except this time there was no candlelight, no flowers, no soft music. Just an awareness of intense feelings. Feelings I knew I hadn't experienced for many years. And all those years ago when I had experienced them, they had never felt like this. And this kind, lovely, funny, wonderful man was evidently feeling the same way. "Am I reading this wrong?" He shyly asked.

All the arguments and reasons as to why this was a very bad idea fled. All the reasons why I should give myself permission to really live and feel and experience whatever I wanted to took over. I was going to celebrate my independence, my newfound spontaneity. I was choosing this in the full awareness that in doing so I was letting myself shrug off my self-imposed mantel of martyrdom and duty. I was allowing myself to be me in the moment without caring what anyone else would think. Or what a good girl would do. Or what was right and proper and appropriate. Sod that. This wasn't about running away from myself into the arms of another. This was about allowing myself to be fully and unapologetically me. All that I desired and deserved. All that I'd been denying myself for years. And so, it happened. Andy and I made love.

Back to that mug of coffee.

Once I was fully awake with that delicious morning mug of coffee in my hands and memories of the previous night coming back to me, my first thoughts were, oh my God, I'm still married! What on earth was I thinking? I should feel really, really guilty. Immediately on the heels of that thought was another: I don't feel the least bit guilty. In fact, I feel bloody wonderful. And with that I tossed off the covers, rose butt naked from the bed, and did a little victory swagger into the bathroom.

Andy and I were shy around each other. It was a giddy sensation of not quite believing what had happened the night before but feeling incredibly happy that it had. We snuck up on to the roof terrace of our Airbnb with our coffees. Andy wanted to show me how the dawn chorus was louder here in Galicia. Galician birds took their choral duties seriously, he said. It was true. We huddled together in the chill morning air happy to listen to their choir practice, as they chirped the day into being, coaxing the sun up so they could warm their dew-soaked feathers in its rays.

I realised Andy and I had done things in reverse. No meeting by chance in a bar, then going on a series of dates where you both bring your 'A' game, revealing the carefully edited and audited best bits of you. Keeping your less palatable bits safely locked away from view. Spending ages trying on and discarding outfits. Making very sure to project your wittiest, wisest, most lovable facade. Like a chef serving up only the most carefully chosen gourmet selection of their tastiest dishes. The luxury high end version of you, not the cut price pick n'mix bag. We'd bypassed all of that. We were already on up close and personal terms with the rawest and realest versions of each other. Andy had certainly seen me at my absolute lowest ebb. He'd witnessed my ugly crying, my insecurities, my grief, my shame, my anger. All the messiest, stinkiest bits of me. And I had been with him on days when he'd been in pain, hungry and knackered. With Andy, what you saw was what you got. I had never met anyone as comfortable in their own skin. Even with that nasty tattoo he wore. He had no need to prove himself in any way, pretence had no foothold, not even a toe's worth on him. Not in a swaggering in yer face sort of way. In a way that said this is who I am, and I like who I am. And I did too. I liked it a lot.

And where did that put me exactly? Nope. I wasn't playing that game. I wasn't going to let my inner prim and proper school prefect out to start laying down the rules and spoiling all the fun. I shut the door firmly in her face. I wasn't going to analyse this; I was simply going to feel and enjoy and love how this felt. I was going to colour outside the lines. I wasn't only going over the edges, I was scribbling all over them. They were no longer even visible to me. No worrying about handing in my homework covered in uncontrolled scribbling, and the possibility of getting a telling off, or even a detention, I just let myself bask in the present moment. Now was fun, vibrant and exciting. And that was more than enough.

Without actually saying it out loud Andy and I both instinctively preferred to keep our liaison a secret. To savour and carry it with us in our backpacks as we floated along the Camino. And not to take it out to share with the others yet. We went downstairs to prepare the family breakfast. Diola and Celine, bleary eyed joined us in the kitchen. "You're both looking chirpy this morning" Diola commented.

Chapter 22
RIDING A STAR

"No one can stop us now

"Cause we are all made of stars."

Moby

As with all families, my little Camino family, had its own quirks and ways. And we accepted and accommodated those ways. In the mornings, especially. We had learnt to flow seamlessly around each other.

Diola was always hyper-organised in every respect. Her backpack would be standing upright and ready for action by the door first thing each morning. I think she might have trained it to get up at dawn and pack itself. Andy would tease her mercilessly, saying he would come round to her flat in Germany one day and mess up her cushions. To which she would try to suppress an involuntary shudder.

Celine would just break into song, not caring if she was in tune or if anyone was listening to her. It was the sort of behaviour most of us keep strictly for the confines of the shower with no one in earshot. There might have been a bit of eye rolling at first, but we adjusted to her ways. And her stuff was always scattered around the place but always miraculously she got herself and her backpack together right at the last minute.

The outwardly seeming bluff and gruff lad, Andy, quietly and unobtrusively needed a bit of meditative time to himself in the mornings. Diola, Celine and I made sure we gave him his space.

One of my quirks was not wanting to know what terrain laid in store for us each day. I preferred just to go with the flow. And tackle the ups and downs as they appeared. But on this morning, I had inadvertently seen Diola's guidebook. It was lying open on the kitchen table, the profile of the day's walk staring back at me. This stage, Ribadeo to Vilanova de Lourenza, had a scary, jagged profile. It looked like we would be up for 29 kms of up and down hill slogs. Oh well. Up and at 'em.

I loved to motor on ahead of the others first thing. The early morning was my favourite time to walk. Particularly on cold frosty mornings like this one was. Everything smelt and felt more alive, the cold air tingled with promise. Of what I couldn't have told you. And I didn't care. As soon as I'd finished my coffee and closed the door of the Airbnb, I hit the Camino at a fast pace. It felt exhilarating to be walking. I felt no need to wait for Andy. I knew he and I had different walking rhythms. He was slow to get started in the mornings and only came into his own around lunchtime. Whereas I bolted out of the gates raring to be off but then I would lose momentum around noon.

Andy was right about one thing. The birds really were louder here in Galicia, I loved that. They kept me company as I took on my first climb of the day. Today I was headed into the heart of rural Galicia. The constantly shifting shades of the blue of the ocean were now exchanged for a sea of greens of equally varied hues. Moment by moment the light show projected by the mercurial skies showcased variations on the theme of green enough to fill its own dictionary. As I walked, I mused over how, when you walk the Camino, you have none of the usual trappings of your life to reflect yourself out to others, no cars, no houses, no jobs, no fancy outfits or uniforms. None of the things you hide yourself behind in your normal daily life come with you on the Camino. All you have is your backpack and what it contains, what it looks like and what it weighs. And your backpack did actually reveal quite a lot about you.

Diola's backpack, for instance, never looked mud spattered no matter the conditions. It was always impeccable. Perfectly packed. It was neither too heavy nor too light. Her walking poles were stowed just so, at the exact same height. She was not a minimalist packer like me. She was always prepared for any eventuality. She was always the one with extra band aids, spare washing line, spare gloves. And then Andy's pack was military in appearance, masculine and made of a tough material that looked as if it would withstand extreme conditions. He said he had spent weeks calculating the precise weights, fibres and brands of his equipment. He had invested a great deal of time and money in getting exactly the right set up. Celine now had her new practical backpack not the uncomfortable, heavy one she had had when Andy and I first met her on the track. She always stuffed it higgledy piggledy right at the last minute. And Boris, my backpack, was of course purple. I'd gone full on minimalist, as was my wont at home too. I preferred to live lightly and unencumbered. Less is more and all that. I had sent back to Granada a few items when I returned from Sarajevo. I now carried only one change of clothes, including one change of underwear and socks, a very few essential toiletries and my sleeping bag. Without water it weighed just over 5kgs. They say you're meant to carry about 10% of your body weight so I was bang on target.

As I tromped through the forest I felt as if I had entered some altered state. The lush vegetation, the relentless greenness of it all was to me like hiking in Wales. The Spain that I had fallen in love with all those years ago was nothing like this. Were it not for the people speaking Spanish and sometimes Gallego, the local language, I wouldn't have known where I was. The scent of eucalyptus was intense. I realised I was now walking through stands of gum trees. I loved the minty clean scent whilst dreading what it implied; the end of the Camino was now within sniffing distance. I chose to focus on the bird song and the beauty of wading through that sumptuous sea of green.

The first coffee stop was sort of obligatory as there was nothing around for a further 10 kms, as was prominently advertised on a sign outside. Despite a constant flow of pilgrims, the place was spotless and welcoming. Painted a buttery golden yellow reflecting the care and warmth exuded by the two lovely women running it. They focused on each individual, giving them their consideration and kindness. Refusing to be rushed or stressed by those waiting. And their attitude was infections. No impatient foot tapping or sighing as you'd sometimes get in other cafes, with people wanting to rapidly refuel and get on. Like so many involved in the Camino these women embodied its spirit and vibrated it out into their lovely establishment so that all were touched by it. Everyone behaved courteously and calmly in here. Pilgrims cleared tables and pulled out chairs for others, inviting them into their midst. And it smelled heavenly too. Of homemade cakes, coffee and cinnamon. I wondered if I could capture some of these Camino scents, bottle and sell it for pilgrims to take home to spray around the house when their Camino longing got the better of them. A blend of eucalyptus, sea breezes, foliage, wet pavement and cafe con leche, with a faint underlying whiff of cow dung. I might be on to something I mused.

It was late in the morning but still pretty cold. We were well into autumn now and it took a while for the heat of the gradually waning sun to take effect. I chose to embrace the coolness of the air and sat outside, happy to be in my own company, curious to see which of my family might catch up with me first. I figured Celine would be way back communing with the trees, Diola probably not too far in front of her. She wasn't saying anything, but we could see that her foot was giving her pain. She always moved at a controlled and steady pace, but she was definitely getting slower. I was pretty sure that Andy would be ahead of them. I was looking out for him among the pilgrims as they came into view. We've all had a 'they' in our lives - wondering where they are and when we will next get to see them. A face that others might not notice in a crowd, but to us it's the one one in sharp focus, all the others just an indistinct blur. A face that generates that lovely but slightly uncomfortable sensation within us when we catch sight of them unexpectedly, as if a tiny frog is leaping lily pads inside our chest. Yes, we've all known that.

I thought back to how Andy and I had got here. I just could never, ever have imagined when we had first met, back at The Twelve Tribes albergue on my first walking day on the Camino that my 'they' would be Andy. Our first impressions of one another had been horrendous. Andy thought me a "a snooty bird" like someone he would expect to see judging the Chelsea Flower Show. And I had thought him a thuggish blight on that beautiful albergue. I had tolerated his presence on the first evening then had quickly capitulated to his infectious sense of humour. His wit was effortless and spot on. We had gradually warmed to one another and became good mates, purely platonic with zero possibility of ever being more to each other than that. It was so refreshing to be in such an entirely uncomplicated friendship with him. He made me laugh so much so that I literally had to beg him to be quiet because I genuinely feared I might spontaneously combust or pee my pants. Or both. He was the perfect dose of genuine compassion, kindness and fun, not a Hallmark version but a down to earth and deeply felt version. He was a hugely independent spirit, a man who marched very much to the beat of his own drum and I found the rhythm he played to be unique and compelling.

I was right, he was the first to arrive. I saw his undisguised look of happiness when he clocked me sitting there. My face reflected back to him his same goofy grin. He had on his Tilley hat and was wearing his lurid green leggings, adding yet another shade of green to the Galician landscape. Let's face it when you walk the Camino carrying your backpack all the way you don't take a fancy wardrobe. You choose the most practical hiking gear without any thought to their possible allure, just their durability. And in Andy's case their carefully calculated weight. Andy had never seen me wear anything but the same 2 sets of clothing. And walking togs are definitely not designed with fashion and flattering lines in mind. I don't think I need to elaborate further.

The next 10 km stretch with no cafes or shops came and went. The Camino's reach falling just short of being able to give a hand up to the poorest of the communities through which it wove. For their sake I hoped for the expansion of the Camino del Norte, even though I loved walking this less travelled route. As I had walked, I had learnt to gauge the prosperity of an area by its horreos. Horreos are ubiquitous along the Camino del Norte. They are little stone storage units, about a metre by two metres, built high up on legs so the rats don't get in and eat all the grain that is stored inside. They have small variations in appearance from The Basque Country, through Cantabria, then Asturias and now here in Galicia. Many of them are now purely decorative, no longer serving the purpose for which they were first built. In Galicia there is a campaign for them to be counted as world heritage sites or objects, so fundamental are they to their sense of identity. Where I was walking now the horreos had begun to look shabby, some caving in on themselves. The weight of unmet expectations and hopes for an economic upturn too heavy to bear, they had given up the ghost. I fancied I could hear them sighing and sagging, giving in to the inevitable. I passed a field which seemed to be growing car tyres, they were the only crop in sight, sewn at random. The saddest thing I saw was a skinny, forlorn looking donkey tied to a post. Not even a good old ear scratch could raise a smile. He seemed, like the corn cribs, to be caving in on himself. I wished I could fill him up with both carrots and cuddles. The former I was sadly lacking in, but I was affluent in the hugs department. But they weren't the currency he craved.

As I passed into more affluent areas, the donkeys were smiling, the corn cribs fancier and the pot-bellied pigs fatter. The biggest and fattest of them all came barrelling over to me as fast as his little trotters could carry him. He moved at an impressive pace for such a big chap. He reminded me of the madreñas - the Asturian clogs, four tiny stilts on each corner holding up his impressive weight. His ears bouncing and flapping, falling over his eyes, as if he too preferred not to know the contours of the terrain over which he travelled. He grunted his approval at a good old ear scratch.

That jagged profile in Diola's guidebook lived up to its threat. To make things a little more challenging it began to rain. There's a good reason why it's so lush and green here. That rain came down with a vengeance reducing visibility to the next few steps ahead of me. I soldiered onwards and upwards. Fortunately, the path was obvious, following the arrows was not an issue. I chose not to stop for shelter as it only made the contrast of stepping back out into the deluge harder to embrace. The walking experience was reduced to one of auditory and olfactory sensations, the thundering of the rain obliterating most sounds. Surrendering to the cold and the soaking made it bearable. Knowing that it was only water and as a friend always said, "We're not made of sugar." I wouldn't melt in it. And if I just kept moving, I could keep relatively warm. Knowing too that I had an Airbnb home for the night, where I would be warm, dry and fed, helped a lot. With my world reduced effectively to a sensory deprivation chamber walking felt dreamlike. Just the sound of my laboured breathing forming a soundtrack along with the thundering bass drumbeat of the rain. The two seemed to synchronise. The rain was so loud I couldn't even hear my feet sloshing, sliding and slogging uphill. I was flooded outside and in by both the water and the overpowering scent of wet earth, eucalyptus and yes that ever present undertone of cow dung.

At one point a new sound entered the mix, I heard what sounded like a monster snuffling and breathing hard straight ahead. I walked into my fears and came across the most immense bull imaginable. Not until I was right up close to it could I make it out. Fortunately, there was a barbed wire fence separating us. He observed me with undisguised disdain for my puniness. He looked as if he had been on a mega weightlifter's course of steroids and hogged the biggest, baddest weights all day long at the gym. He had no discernible neck. He was just one monumental mass of muscle. I didn't dare take out my phone to take his photo, I would have needed my underwater camera to do so. I had no idea if any of the others were behind, ahead or even beside me. I just trusted that each of us was gradually wading and weaving our way to our home for the night.

I was mightily relieved to cross over the picturesque little bridge into Lourenza. I was the first to arrive, the keys were in a safety box by the front door. I willed my numb fingers into action to punch in the numbers. Andy, Diola and Celine all gradually appeared, each of us depositing as much of our drenched garb as possible in the hallway. The Airbnb soon dried and lifted our spirits. It was modern but managed to be both roomy and yet still snug and cosy. The thick brick walls were so comforting. I was happy not to be standing shivering outside a communal shower in an albergue waiting my turn with my, still damp from the previous day, handkerchief sized towel clutched to me trying to maintain some minimal sense of privacy.

The lashing abundance of hot water cascading from the power shower worked its magic. I was soon revived and ready for a pre-dinner reccy. Andy had offered to make a veggie lasagne, pasta free and therefore gluten free. I had no idea how he would do it, but I knew he was more than up to the task. I offered to help him get in what he needed. Shopping done at the nearby supermarket, we didn't feel inclined to wander into the town centre. It was still bucketing down. So, we hopped into the convenient little bar next door. We weren't really all that interested in seeing the town anyway. We were far more interested in focusing on each other. We were admittedly acting like love struck teenagers but as Andy rightly pointed out, why should they be the ones to have all the fun?

We headed back to the family home for the night to prepare dinner. Still keeping 'us' a secret. Still enjoying the feeling of being a little naughty. Still savouring that delicious feeling of being our own little self-contained constellation. Riding our star to Santiago.

Chapter 23
JUST ME

"It's about waking up in the morning and saying:

No matter what gets done and how much is done and how it's done,

I'm enough and I'm worthy of belonging and love and joy."

Brene Brown

We stood and looked back up at the Airbnb flat we had just vacated in Lourenza. We had pulled the dead bolted door shut and left the keys inside as instructed. Celine, who had been the last to grab her clothes from the line, had assured us that she had checked that all the windows were closed. She looked a little sheepish as we pointed up to the wide-open windows in the galeria. The 'galeria' is a sort of walled and windowed balcony common to Galician homes. Thankfully the torrential rain of the previous day had poured itself dry during the night and we had been able to air our gear there before we left

I love these galerias. You can sit snugly inside, with your hands wrapped around a cuppa, and experience the rain lashing fiercely down towards you. It feels like being inside a giant car wash with massive

185

bucketfuls of water constantly being hurled at you. Occasionally instinctively ducking when a particularly big wave bears down in your direction. And on sunny days clothes are hung up there to dry. I messaged the owner to let them know of our transgression. It wasn't an issue. Someone would be there soon to prepare for the next visitors. I saw Diola shaking her head and muttering to herself. Andy didn't look too impressed either.

I wondered if this might be a Camino 'hump day'; a phenomenon I'd witnessed accompanying the Gucci Camino groups. All peace and harmony to begin with, everyone bringing their best selves to the party. Then about halfway through the trip, a touch of disharmony would always enter the fray. People no longer feeling the need to be on their best behaviour and getting a bit snippy with each other. Things levelled out again after that. Admittedly a little later into the journey than usual, but this might be our Camino hump day.

I knew it wouldn't last but lengthened my stride, or rather increased my trot and forged ahead alone into the brisk but clear morning. I was headed to Abadin, 25 kms away. I was meandering through small agricultural communities. I was surrounded by satisfyingly solid stone constructions at every turn. It felt comforting to be walking amongst them. Giving a fixed and firm basis on which I could depend. A solid, trustworthy structure supporting me. Around each corner a stone cross, bridge, chapel, farmhouse or horreo. Rough-hewn and reliable.

You know that magic trick when you pull a tablecloth off so fast that the objects on it remain stationary? I had that sensation of the cloth of Spain being relentlessly tugged out from beneath me. Try as I might to plant my feet firmly on it to hold it in place, a bit more slipped out from under me each time I lifted my foot to take a step. The cloth of The Basque Country had gone, Cantabria had gone, Asturias had just been pulled over the edge of the table. Now I was planting my feet with great intent on the material of Galicia. Stomping it into place. Anchoring it with my weight. Because if the last bit of Camino cloth was whipped out from under me, what would I have left to stand on? I wasn't yet ready to tread the bare boards of life alone. Even though the terrain within me was feeling less convoluted, and I was experiencing far less grief and anger, able to observe and enjoy the scenery around me again, still I felt the need to imbibe a bit more camino wisdom and warmth. I increased my resolve to just walk and breathe and trust. Accepting that there would be an endpoint, that with the final tug of the cloth, Santiago would topple off the table too. But also acknowledging that I could choose to view that endpoint as a beginning.

I was relieved that by the time we regrouped in Mondoñedo,'hump day', or rather 'hump morning', was already behind us. We all congregated at a cafe opposite the imposing cathedral. This was the only place on the Camino del Norte, other than Santiago, that was home to a cathedral. After our coffees, the others headed straight back to the path. But I figured I should at least take a quick look in. But as soon as I set foot inside, I had the same sensation wash over me that I always got inside such grand ecclesiastical constructions. That of a slight revulsion at all the glitz and gold. I couldn't help it. It just happened. These were the same feelings that I had had at my confirmation classes all those years ago, prior to my sister's wedding. Confirmation, yes, but of the fact that the church just wasn't the place for me to feel the peace, love and joy that I longed to experience. I let

187

the heavy oak door creak shut behind me. Envying those pilgrims on their knees in prayer. Part of me so wished that I could wholeheartedly join them.

I had heard quite a lot about this town, Mondoñedo. I'd been told it had a particular charm and beauty. As I pottered happily around its streets and the arcaded square opposite the cathedral, I had to agree. It had its own unique flavour, including some lovely old-fashioned shops. With an Art Deco feel to them. The town felt energised and forward thinking. There were artisans' workshops and cafes. But it wasn't in the least a parody of itself as other cutesy towns have become, with every second building a hotel or bar. This was a very real and alive and lived in place. One I would like to return to and linger a while longer. But for now, the Camino called.

Shortly after leaving the town, I came across a Camino marker showing a Camino complementaria, an alternative route, to my destination for the night. Well, wasn't that what I was doing here? Looking for a different path? So, I took it. I relished the liberating feeling of not knowing where exactly I was but that I was on the way. It felt fitting for my current situation. In Galicia they count down the remaining kilometres to Santiago on the 'mojones' the stone markers. On this alternative path there were no distances marked on them, but at least you were assured that you were on your way to your goal. Trusting that the path would be revealed to you as long as you just kept on moving forward.

After a while even those stone markers petered out. But I chose to trust that I was on the right path. I was following a distinct trail. I chose not to worry about it. I sat and took a break in a field, turned my face up to the sun. I placed Boris behind me, leaning back into him, exchanging roles, letting him be the one to take my weight for a change. I munched on a banana, and some raisins and almonds. And I realised that I felt completely content. Just me n' Boris. Not entirely sure where we were but knowing we were on our way. I could just relax, let go of the controls and enjoy the view. I contemplated with awe how everything had lined up for me to get to this place, lying here contented. Even before I'd left home. What had initially seemed like such a spanner in the works, having to separate myself legally and financially from Pedro, had been my first step on this path to freedom. With my new self-employed status, I was completely independent of him. The Camino had worked its magic before I had even set foot on it.

Then I heard a sound that scared me. A snuffling sound coming from behind a tall hedge on the path in the direction that I would soon have to take. I thought of the bull I'd seen the previous day. Surely not. I listened again. This sounded more like a dog. And a big one. There was no one around for miles. If it was a big guard dog let loose, I was royally screwed. Why hadn't I stayed on the main path with all the others? I reminded myself that I had chosen to trust and that meant not backing down at the first challenge. I could do this. I stood with what I hoped a dog would sense as resolve and strength and walked around the corner. Straight into Celine!

 I was both surprised and thankful that it was her. What on earth had she been doing to make all that noise? She nonchalantly said she had just been doing the necessary. What I'd imagined to be a rabid dog scuffling in the dirt and breathing laboriously had in fact been a French woman relieving herself in the middle of a field. Celine felt no trace of embarrassment. She had a much more liberated approach to all bodily functions than me. I would rather pee my pants than be caught with them around my ankles. And I always took long and laborious detours deep into the woods to assure myself of privacy. Celine would drop them wherever was convenient to her, not caring who might see. She took no notice of my shocked expression. How could I think that she was a dangerous dog? She found that hilarious! I loved how lightly she approached life.

A battered old pick-up truck came along. The driver, a local farmer, offered to give us a lift back to the main Camino. The day was getting on, so we figured why not? About a kilometre further on we saw the familiar brim of a Tilley hat by the side of the path. Andy was lying under his hat taking a nap. He was more than a little surprised to see us. The driver wasn't quite as enthusiastic about picking him up as he had been with us, but he agreed, and soon deposited us by the side of the main route.

In Abadin we stayed in a private albergue. Sarah and Richard, who were still a day ahead of us, had recommended it. It was brand spanking new and shiny. Nothing was too much trouble for the hospitalero who received us beautifully. He was obviously and justifiably proud of these wonderful new premises. Showers were piping hot. The breakfast area would not have looked out of place in an upmarket high street bistro. We were invited to help ourselves to cake and pastries. Including gluten free choices. We had a dorm to ourselves. Just 6 bunks. With low level lighting cleverly concealed right next to the pillows.

That night we had dinner at a restaurant opposite. The owner was surprised when we asked for Pacharan to round off our meal. Not the norm here in Galicia. 'Huh! I had two pilgrims in here last night who asked for it too," he said. 'Let me see would that have been an extremely fit looking Canadian couple by any chance?' I asked. He was surprised that we knew them. He went on to say that they had looked so disappointed when he said he didn't stock Pacharan that he nipped over the road to the supermarket and bought in a bottle. He assumed that it would then sit on his shelf for years.

The Camino always provides. Even Pacharan.

Chapter 24

PULPO FERIA REVISITED

"Take a lover that looks at you like maybe you are magic."

Frida Kahlo

Five weeks ago, the vast expanse of the Camino del Norte had lain unfurled seemingly endlessly before me. Now there remained only a tiny fragment measuring just over 100 kms to go. The closer we got to Santiago, the more Diola was hurting. She had a recurring problem with a tendon. She never made a fuss. She soldiered on, head down gritting her teeth, carefully planting each foot. But it was obvious to Celine, Andy and me that she was in a lot of pain. Her injury was the type that could heal with rest. Lots of rest. Which wasn't an option now for her. She had her flight back to Germany booked for the 15th of October. It was now the 7th. If she wanted to get her Compostela, the certificate that told the world she had walked the Camino, she would have to walk every step of the last 100 kms. Normally that would have been a piece of cake for her but now it was looking increasingly doubtful.

Finding Love On The Camino

As we walked from Abadin that morning, I kept seeing a flyer for a new albergue called O'Xistral. Something about it drew me to it. I knew I had to stay there. Which made no sense given that it was only about 6 kms away. But I felt so drawn to it that I knew I had no choice. I tentatively broached this with the others. Diola looked mightily relieved at the prospect of such a short walk and the chance to rest. Andy and Celine, always flexible, agreed we could take a look and see if we could make it work.

We arrived there mid-morning. We realised straight away that this was no normal albergue. As with our previous night's accommodation, it was very obviously brand new. The owners had just finished building the albergue of their dreams. But unlike the super modern albergue of the previous night in Abadin, this albergue was made of rough-hewn stone, with a traditional slate roof. Everything about it spoke of deep pride and love of all things Galician. Exquisite attention to detail was reflected in every corner of the building, in every lovingly placed stone, in the enticing little inglenook next to the roaring fire. The whole placed hummed with the love with which it had been dreamt into existence. Celine and Andy were won over by the magic of the place. Our arrival, so early in the day, wasn't a problem. We were given our own space with bunks for the four of us.

It was a glorious autumn day, the sun was out but not searingly hot, the perfect temperature to sit and soak in the warmth and the beauty of the albergue grounds. I lay in lush grass and let the waves of appreciation for this day, for these friends, for this little piece of paradise ripple through me. How had I got to be so blessed? No, not questioning it. I was claiming it all including the little secret that Andy and I shared. We were still behaving like lovestruck teenagers. It felt a little giddy, a little naughty, and so much bloody fun. Floating around in our own private little bubble of joy. Throughout the day more pilgrims trickled in and looked around in awe. So many felt drawn to stay but not all could, having already made other plans and reservations. We were amongst the fortunate few who didn't have to walk on casting longing lingering glances back. It felt like a true Camino gift.

Offers to help with preparing dinner were appreciated but politely refused. We were allowed however to help set the tables. I recognised the big copper pot placed at the end of one of the tables. Were we going to have a Queimada? After all Galicia is the land of witches and magic. The Queimada is a traditional ritual to dispel evil spirits and invite in the good. It's not the sort of ritual you order with your dinner. It's done when the time feels right. When the company is fitting. When the stars are aligned. I hoped they would be that evening. In this microcosm of magic my wishes came true.

As with everything about the Albergue O'Xistral, our dinner was a fitting reflection of Galician culture. An array of the delicious traditional fare of the area was served. And after we had helped clear away the plates, the owner, Pepe, began preparing for the Queimada. He asked for a volunteer to translate the words, looking at me as he did so. How did he know I would jump at the chance? The lights were turned down low. Liquor was poured into the great copper pot and set alight. The ceremony of the Queimada was commencing. It wasn't to be rushed; it had its own process. We were transfixed by the flames and the sense of ceremony. As the flames leapt higher, the remaining lights were switched off, the Queimada was stirred, and we were all drawn into that circle of light. I translated Pepe's words almost in a trance. He was asking for the bad spirits to be kept at bay and invoking the good ones to come to our aid. All our negative thoughts and experiences were purified in that fire, and the light of the good spirits were called forward to now illuminate our lives.

When it was all over Pepe received a phone call. It was pretty late by now, the sun had long since gone down. He beckoned me over to speak with the pilgrim who evidently spoke very little Spanish. Within moments I realised that the person on the phone was an Italian German speaking girl called Sabine who was walking the Camino with her lovely little terrier Max. We had met up with her often over the last few weeks. She seemed to have manifested the one terrier who wasn't that energetic or keen on walking and so she ended up pushing him most of the way in a specially adapted dog 'pram'. She camped out many nights in an insubstantial tent as the municipal albergues didn't accept dogs and not many of the private ones did either. I explained to Pepe that she was looking for a place to sleep for the night for both her and Max. He said he couldn't have the dog in the dormitory, but he would be happy for Sabine and Max to sleep downstairs next to the fire if it was OK with everyone else? Which, of course, it was. They arrived twenty minutes later, exhausted and cold and were received with a warm meal and a more than welcome place to rest their heads for the night. Sabine was immensely grateful. We were all so happy to have spared her yet another cold night out by herself. She was soon snoring happily on the long comfortable couch with Max curled up in a furry warm ball at her feet.

I was reluctant for this evening to come to an end. But I knew the owners had an even earlier start than me the next day. They had to prepare for the next group of pilgrims fortunate enough to stay here.

I made my way towards my bunk, but Andy intercepted me. He handed me my jacket and whispered to me to come outside. He had prepared our sleeping mats and sleeping bags under the stars. We could lie snug and warm and take in the performance of the brightly lit night sky. On cue, the moon loomed from behind the clouds. We heard voices from behind us. Diola and Celine were dragging out their sleeping bags too. Which was perfect. It was too spectacular a show to keep to ourselves.

The next morning Diola was crestfallen and quiet. Her ankle was so sore she was unable to walk at all. Celine immediately offered to stay behind and be her nurse maid. Diola was not entirely convinced of Celine's aptitude for this role. But I was through with subjugating my wants and desires. So instead of selflessly offering to stay with Diola as former me would have done I wished them well and Andy and I were out that door before she could utter "Don't leave me!" We were off to the town of Vilalba. The night before Pepe had told me there would be a pulpo, octopus, feria there today.

Unencumbered by Boris I couldn't resist a bit of a run. I knew Andy would catch me up at some point, probably over a cafe con leche. It was a gorgeous Camino morning with bright sunshine accentuating every hue of autumn. The Camino looked like an overly enthusiastic five-year-old had been let loose with a paint box and daubed it all with impossible shades of red, yellow and orange, the colours were so ridiculously bold and bright. Unseasonably, it hadn't rained in this part of Galicia for days and I crunched my way through piles of crispy leaves, laughing like that five-year-old. Who couldn't resist leaping into piles of crackling leaves that demanded to be crunched underfoot? The trees enclosed me in brightly tinted tunnels. I felt like I was running in

197

an autumnal Galician snow globe as the breezes shook a smattering of brightly coloured leaves down around me.

After 10 kms I was lured by the sign for a cafe, just off the Camino. I was pretty sure that Andy would be drawn in by it too and probably catch up with me there. And he did indeed. We had cafe con leche on this beautiful autumn day with the sun on our faces as we basked in contented silence together. A silence completely unlike any silence I had experienced before. Certainly, totally unlike the silences that had marked so many of the days of my marriage.

When we reached Vilalba we followed our noses to the site of the pulpo feria. A full on traditional affair. No tourist trappings. But all were welcome. Vast copper pots steamed. Trestle tables covered in white paper were lined up in rows. They were anchored in place with squat, square shaped bottles of local wine. Mob capped women in checked aprons wiped the sweat from their brows, as they wielded thick wooden platters of octopus. The smell was intoxicating. No need for a menu. Just pulpo, potatoes and wine. What more could you want? We looked for empty spaces on the crowded benches.

Straight away I had flashes of the pulpo feria with Pedro in Bilbao. The mud and the rain of that day seemed another lifetime ago. I had been shy and hesitant about imposing on such a local affair. I remember being anxious that Pedro was doing the wrong thing by insisting that we join in the festivities. I felt sure he was putting others and us in an awkward position. As I recalled that time it felt like I was watching another person, someone I used to hang out with. Frankly, she felt like a bit of a bore. Her very concerns about imposing on others would in fact make them feel uncomfortable. Everyone was only focused on having a jolly good time with family and friends. And with strangers, or as they would probably see her, if she would allow it, new friends. Any worries that she wouldn't be welcomed had only every existed in her head. That school report card that caused her anxiety - "Debbie is always the perfect guest, the perfect wife, the perfect pilgrim…."Ugggh I much preferred me now.

A couple of pilgrims beckoned us towards them. As we drew closer, I realised that I recognised their faces. I hadn't seen them for weeks. It was Miriam and Mario! They were the last people I had expected to see again. We hadn't seen them since the monastery of Zenarrruza before I left the Camino for Sarajevo. Back then I had watched the tussle for the affections of the easy going, good looking Italian guy, Mario, play out. Miriam, the older of the two women, who was Spanish with an air of determination and toughness had won out over the younger, softer German woman, Klara. Mario asked where my husband, the Argentinian was. I told him that his guess was as good as mine. He was taken aback by my honesty. I couldn't see why he should be. He turned his attention back to the pulpo but Mariam was desperate to hear more. I had heard the expression 'her eyes grew wide as saucers' but didn't know this phenomenon could actually happen. It did to Miriam. She was fascinated by this turn of events and wanted to hear all the details. As I told all, I was pleasantly surprised to find that all trace of sadness over the end of my marriage had left me. It was replaced with relief. The charade was over, no more painful procrastination. What awaited me after this could stay right where it was. I sat and indulged in the food and the wine with the local families out to thoroughly enjoy themselves. Uncomplicated enjoyment of delicious simply prepared food. No thought to dashing back to the office or taking their pulpo to go.

Chapter 25

BURSTING THE BALLOON

"Vibrational flow is as natural to your world

as sunshine and air.

Your flow of positive and negative is

your source of expansion, savor it!"

David Strickel

The next morning Diola said her foot was feeling better. Or perhaps she simply did not want to be left for another day to the tender mercies of nurse Celine. So, we left the warmth and comfort of albergue O'Xistral behind us. Pepe, the albergue owner, had arranged for his dad to give us a lift to our start point for that morning. He would leave us just past Vilalba, where Andy and I had walked to the previous day. His dad was a lovely chap. He obviously set great store on being spiffily attired. He turned up in a battered leather jacket and aviator sunglasses. He had a distinct air of Clint Eastwood as the Galician morning mist swirled about him.

Finding Love On The Camino

The morning mist turned into heavy fog as we walked. There was an otherworldly feeling about this part of the Camino. The tree tunnelled lanes that had been so brightly illuminated the previous day now felt menacing and oppressive in the misty gloom. Closing in on us as we made our way along them. The spider web festooned hedges, the spiky witchy trees and the low hanging fog made us instinctively walk slightly hunched over, protecting ourselves from unknown forces lurking just out of sight.

We walked through abandoned villages that made us pick up our pace. We grouped together so as not to be tainted by their air of sad defeat. There was a ghostly feel to those empty, crumbling facades. I felt as if I was being watched from behind them. As if something was trying to lure me off the path to stay a while with them, to make them feel less alone, less abandoned to their fate. As if invisible hands were clawing at my clothes to tug me back. Houses with shutters swinging on hinges and doors hanging off looked as if they had been beaten up, kicked around and left for dead. Although I hated to see the kilometres counting down I did not to choose to stop the hands of time here. We marched briskly on and through.

Even the hamlets that were still semi-occupied had a defeated air about them. Women as stooped and gnarled as the witchy trees scuttled across the farmyards with battered buckets of animal feed in a pointless attempt to stave off the inevitable. Here no gangs of giggling children kicked up their heels, trotting alongside us chanting, 'Buen Camino', as we passed. Even the chickens were skinny and ancient. Their forlorn eyes seemed to follow us as we walked past. The chained bony mastiff hounds didn't even bother to growl, let alone leap, at passing strangers. There was nothing much left for them to protect here. An air of resignation hung low like the mist over their heads. The fog had leached out of the scene any last vestige of colour or life. We passed through a series of similar sepia-coloured photos that would soon to be tossed onto the bonfire, their edges curling in on themselves before being consumed in the flames of time. Cruelly, the only structure of substance in the area was the gleaming white wedding cake tiered cemetery. Large and imposing. This was evidently the final resting place for all the villagers in the surrounding area. They would eventually be housed here in more solid surroundings. I shivered and increased my pace.

Today we entered the final 100 kms of the Camino. A momentous occasion on any Camino. From there on in, the end is undeniably within reach. Much as I might wish otherwise. On the Camino del Norte, unlike on the Camino Frances, there was no official 100 km marker to accentuate this important milestone. In fact, we walked right on without realising we were already into the home stretch. We only realised this when we reached 99. 7 km marker. At my insistence we retraced our steps back to the 100.4 km marker, to take the obligatory photo.

The fog had lifted by late morning and our spirits along with it. And it turned into another flawless, crisp, sunny autumn day. We crossed over the most perfectly formed medieval bridge imaginable. You could practically see the knight in shining armour clip clopping across it, lance in hand. And if you blurred your vision a little, out of the corner of your eye you could catch brief glimpses of ancient pilgrims trudging sore footed over it.

Close by, just off the path, was a tiny chapel. Nothing remarkable, but something about this place made me stop and walk around its perimeter. Something there called me to it and had me rest a while, Boris by my side, with my back pressed against its warm mossy wall. It was transmitting something of importance to me. I could feel it. I had no idea as to what that was, but I felt its positive pull. It purged me of the jagged thoughts and feelings of those abandoned villages.

That day we were headed to an albergue named Witericus, on an alternative Camino path. It had been recommended to us by our friends at the previous albergue. Although nothing could compare with the splendour of O'Xistral, it was a beautiful little stone dwelling. Comprised of just one small dormitory with a lovely sun filled, glass walled, reading room attached. Leather bound books lined its walls. And a battered green leather chair invited you to curl up with a book. This albergue was a haven for cats. They wound between your legs, butted you with their soft heads, purred their way up onto your lap. The word had evidently got around that any abandoned waifs or strays would be welcomed here. They were well used to pilgrims and accepted their petting and being cradled as their right, even their duty. Small warm feline hospitaleros offering additional comfort and love to the weary pilgrim. One more magical evening on the Camino. Pre-dinner glass of wine in hand, no house to clean, no bills to pay, no work to worry over. Completely relaxed in both mind and body. Nowhere I would rather be. Andy and I sloped off unnoticed and silently shared the sunset. No words necessary.

Reaching Sobrado dos Monxes the next afternoon meant that we had only one day left on the Camino del Norte route before it merged with the Camino Frances. At dinner in a local restaurant that evening, we looked around at the, by now, familiar faces of the other Camino families around us. We were on at least nodding terms with most of them. Tomorrow would be a different story. Tomorrow we would arrive at Arzua with its influx of Camino families that had chosen the path more travelled. The French Way. We would no longer walk amongst the exclusive wandering tribe of the northern route. I wondered how it would feel to share our path with faces unknown to us. To stop for coffee and no longer automatically recognise the doting Dutch couple in the corner, the trio of athletic young German guys, the grey trousered old Spanish men brigade. We had formed our own shorthand to describe them, and they had probably done the same for us. I wondered how we might be described amongst them. I smiled with fondness upon them all.

Tomorrow the air would slowly start to be released from our Camino bubble. From there on in it would start to deflate and lose its form. From Arzua a paltry 38.7 kms would separate us from Santiago. Leaving us with 48,750 steps left to take. We had started off in Irun, measuring distances in terms of weeks left. We now measured time in days remaining. Soon we would be measuring it in terms of hours left on the Camino. Then minutes. Until even those ran out. It physically pained me to contemplate it. I incanted my now well-worn mantra silently to myself; 'I'm still here. I'm still on the Camino'. But even this talisman was powerless to stop time.

Chapter 26

NORTE NO MORE

"The universe is full of magical things

patiently waiting for our wits to grow sharper."

Eden Phillpotts

In Sobrado dos Monxes I shyly 'came out' to Diola and Celine about my changed relationship with Andy. It was early morning as we were stripping the beds before leaving our Airbnb. My allocated single bed hadn't been slept in. My conscience would not allow me to waste resources washing bedsheets that had not been slept in. Diola threw me one of her famous eye rolls, "You really thought we didn't know?" she asked. Celine fell about laughing. "It was so, so obvious," she said. She thumped me triumphantly on the arm. They both gave their very heartfelt approval and encouragement. They 'officially' announced the news to Sarah and Richard via the Camino group WhatsApp. And here I was, so certain that Andy and I had been subtle and secretive about it.

That morning I had to get myself to a bank to transfer the rent for my flat in Granada. My flat. No longer 'our' flat. I liked how that sounded.

My flat. I had found a branch of my bank in a village 8 kms into the day's walk. Everything in Spain took longer. I knew I would be waiting in line for a good half hour or so, while the bank clerk discussed local affairs with customers and then went off for a coffee break. So, I set off at a trot arranging to meet up with the others for coffee when I was through. Road walking was becoming more frequent now as we got closer to Santiago. Today was a mix of forest trails and tarmac, my feet were accustomed to it all. The weather was still being unseasonably kind to us. The morning started out misty but that burnt away by mid-morning.

The communities were a lot more affluent around here. The horreos were well tended, some even painted. In England the neighbours judge each other by the state of their lawns; trim and neatly manicured or unkempt and weed infested. Here keeping up with the Jones's, or rather the Rodriguez's, seemed to be a competition as to who had the neatest, shiniest horreo in town. Here, even the hay was stacked in neat and tidy bales in the fields. Dogs from tiny terriers to well fed mastiff hounds hurled themselves with great intent at the metal fencing as I passed. In this part of Galicia there was plenty for them to protect. Nearing the village, I was to stop at, I came across one of my very favourite things, a whole field daubed in poster paint Camino bright yellow, sunflowers. God, I love sunflowers. Even though we were nearing mid-October they were in full smiling bloom, heads held high, beaming with joy. As, of course, was I. So much so that I could not contain myself. I burst into song as I rushed to greet them. I did not care who else was around or if I might give them a fright. It just did not get better than this.

When I arrived at the bank not only had it opened promptly but there was no one else in line. I was dealt with quickly and efficiently. I was in and out the door within minutes. Wow! As with the post office back in Laredo when we'd sent back Andy's camping gear. So much for my predictions. I then found the perfect cafe to wait for the others. Right on the path. It had a tiny, tidy flower-lined terrace. I sat and observed my fellow Camino del Norte pilgrims as they came by. I greeted as many as possible that morning, knowing this would be the last day when I would see so many familiar faces. We all shared at least a nod, and many stopped for a chat.

Andy was first to arrive, then Celine, which was odd, she was usually the last to straggle in. Neither had seen Diola. We waited patiently. Eventually we saw her defeated form, dragging itself towards us. We rushed to take her pack. She slumped into a chair and a tear slid down her cheek. Her Camino was over she said. The pain in her foot was so great she could not walk another step. She was gutted. She was usually so self-composed in every way. It was painful to see her crumble like this. It didn't matter how many kilometres she had already walked, the official certificate that proved that she had walked at all, the Compostela, would only be awarded to her if she walked every step of the last 100 kms. I didn't know if that certificate was important to her, I suspected it wouldn't be of huge significance but, of course, enjoying her last few days on the Camino and walking under her own steam into the cathedral square was hugely important to her. No wonder she was crushed.

I arranged for a taxi to come pick her up and take her directly to the Airbnb flat we had rented for our stay in Arzua. Celine offered to go with her. The chap who had rented us the Airbnb flat had insisted that we should take it for two nights. He'd said that the Camino was very busy and it would be easy for us to take buses backwards and forwards between the Camino towns. I had thought maybe it was just a clever ploy on his part to make his life easier. Now, for Diola's sake, I was extremely grateful I had accepted his offer.

Arriving at Arzua was an even greater shock than I had imagined. I sat waiting for Andy at the main crossroads into town. Wherever I turned there was an army of backpacks on the move. Judging by the noise levels and animated hand gestures, even from afar, I could tell most of them were Spaniards. Why were there so many pilgrims? I tried to figure out the date. Of course, it was the weekend of the 12th of October, 'el dia de la Hispanidad'. It was the nationwide holiday celebrating Columbus's discovery of the Americas. Not brilliant timing for us arriving here. Everywhere would be rammed. Thankfully, we were sorted.

Andy and I took off on our now obligatory pre-dinner reccy to enjoy a drink alone and find the best place in town to eat. We found the ideal spot, tucked down an inconspicuous side street. It was old fashioned, plain and unpretentious. When I saw that the men at the bar were wearing street sweepers' overalls, I knew we had hit gold. They always know the best places to eat. A huge old manual cash register hunkered down on the bar top. Its wooden drawer slamming shut with a satisfying thwump each time it was used. A complex strata of lottery tickets and bar bills from years past hung behind the bar. Next to them, an old, mottled mirror, like a face covered in age spots. It reflected the starkly furnished room. A calendar dated 1998 hung alongside the mirror. A dominoes game was going on in the corner. One that had doubtlessly been played out for decades. The outcome irrelevant. Life here was about maintaining a sense of tradition and continuity. The turn of the century nearly twenty years prior had barely been registered. We perched ourselves on the tall metal stools alongside the street sweepers. Our thighs were pressed together, heads close. We still had the prospect of the uncomplicated joyful rinse and repeat of Camino life cocooning us. For just two more days.

+++++++++

The next day Diola had no choice. She had to have a rest day. Her ankle was so sore she was only able to hobble from one room to another. Andy and I had got in provisions for her from the local supermarket. She had plenty to eat and drink. Plenty to read. There was good wifi connection. She insisted that she was fine. Celine decided to stay behind as well. She claimed she needed to have a 'beauty day' so she would be looking her best for her upcoming rendezvous with a certain Santiago de Compostela. Or possibly she was thoughtfully keeping Diola company. Either way, it was just Andy and me togging up for our last full day on the Camino. Boris looked slightly miffed to be left behind. But it was too good an opportunity to miss, a day's walking unencumbered. We would return by bus in the afternoon.

The Camino del Norte had taught me to never miss the opportunity to replenish my caffeine levels. We stopped at the first open cafe we saw. Soy milk lattes, oversized, brightly coloured coffee mugs, tempting pastries, even gluten free pastries. They were sure switched on in this town. Everything a 21st century pilgrim requires in a coffee stop. Hitting the trail, we soon realised that we could have had our pick of a myriad coffee stops just like that one. This last section of the

Camino, where the Camino del Norte and the Camino Frances blend, was a different beast altogether to what we had become used to. I'd been so all consumed by the Norte that I'd completely forgotten how, particularly this last stretch of the French Camino, catered generously to every flavour of pilgrim.

Andy and I started off together but soon our well-worn pattern set in. Without the anchoring weight of Boris on my back, my walking shoes were jet propelled. But there was just one problem. There were too many pilgrims. There wasn't just a swell in the number of people on the path. There was a whole tidal wave, a tsunami of pilgrims. It was impossible to outrun them, to get ahead of the wave. I had no choice but to be swept along by the tide. If I or any of the other pilgrim had envisaged a day of quiet contemplation and communion with the spirit of the Camino, we were shit out of luck. And we just had to get over ourselves and go with it. I gave up excusing myself as I scooted past groups strung out all over the path. I would have spent the whole morning apologising. The vast majority of the groups were Spaniards taking advantage of their national holiday. The Spanish are not a quiet, tidy and orderly people by nature. Whereas Brits would have formed an orderly queue to allow overtaking, the Spaniards sprawled across the path, oblivious to those in their wake, flailing sticks and arms as they walked and laughed. Claiming it as their own. And it was in fact theirs. Their country. Their special weekend. Their Camino. Whatever form that took. I reminded myself of the most basic of Camino tenets 'Don't judge'.

And it was so tempting to judge these weekend walkers as less than us. We who had walked all the way from Irun. Well, most of it. And there were those who had come from even further afield, walking out of their front doors in Holland, France, or even more remote starting points and who were now taking their last steps to Santiago. Surely, we the chosen few, deserved our own special path? Like the priority boarding line. First class pilgrims as opposed to these coach class tourists. Those thoughts were undeniably there. I was disappointed that after all this time on the Camino I had not been cleansed of my need to categorise and compare. But then I remembered that I had given up on being saintly. I could either choose to have a frustrating day playing dodge the pilgrim, or I could enter into the festive feel of the day. I could dance and sing with them, chat at high volume and celebrate along with them. So, I ran, and I jumped in the piles of crunchy leaves. I Buen Camino'd and high fived my way along. Weaving in and out of the crowds. Sharing a moment and a smile and a laugh with many. I was aware that all too soon decisions would have to be made as to my future. But for now, I was trusting that in the right moment I would know what to do, and what I truly wanted. It felt bloody wonderful to no longer be stuck. I was instead going to make deliberate and brave decisions. That was how I was going to honour my Camino.

The trail still followed forest paths and wound its way through well-tended villages whose local economy was boosted by the constant supply of passing trade. But it also ran alongside motorways, crossing them in places, a reminder of the faster, less benign world to which we would soon all have to return. I could feel the tumultuous emotions that millions of pilgrims had left behind along this section. I was most certainly not the first person to be walking with such conflicting feelings of simultaneous deep joy and deep sadness at the fast-approaching end. And I certainly wouldn't be the last. This was reflected in the evident compulsion to make a mark, to leave some physical imprint that proved that they had once been here. To somehow express the enormity of their experience on the Camino in a way that could actually be seen and touched. Claiming this moment, grabbing it with both hands and planting it on the path. Resulting in a profusion of graffiti on every available surface. Including the stone mile markers. Though it made me wince to witness their defacement I could appreciate many of the sentiments. Such as 'Va vers toi meme' - Walk towards yourself. OK, a bit cheesy but as Andy had said to me the previous day, this is what we were all doing on the Camino. Walking back into the arms of ourselves. He was not one for expressing Hallmark sentiments. And it hadn't felt as such when he'd said it. It had felt very bloody true.

And I totally got this visceral need to leave something of yourself behind here. Walls were plastered with names and dates, in one place a wall of bottles with people's names on them had been built. Some containing messages. A message in a bottle to be found by future selves maybe. To remind them of who they had become here. I think many were afraid of losing what they had found on the Camino once they were sucked back into their old lives. Would they succumb to their former patterns, their old values and ways of being? Would this whole walk serve as a temporary Camino patch that would peel off and drop to the floor?

Stallholders had set up along the way to capitalise on those raw emotions and the need for a memento to take back through to the other side of the looking glass with you, as a talisman. Anything to recapture the essence of the Camino. Hoping that it could be stored in a scented candle, in a key ring, in a patch on your backpack. Cashing in on the fact that we no longer had to worry about every extra gram of weight as we only had to carry our backpacks for a further 45,000 paces. A feeding frenzy of Camino tat ensued. A prominently placed fridge magnet might exert a pull strong enough to counteract that of our daily lives, made heavy with obligations, bills, commitments. We were all desperate to take home some little bit of the Camino to hang on to by our fingernails when life was threatening to sweep us away in its torrent.

I noticed many for sale signs on half abandoned buildings, fixer uppers that could become the next new albergue. Most of us must have had at least a fleeting dream of returning to live on the Camino. The local property owners and real estate agents sought to stoke the fires of that dream. They were fanning the flames with the tempting suggestion that we could actually do it. Whilst the iron was still hot, they were taking their chance to strike. While we were still raw and vulnerable and suggestible. Knowing that once the backpack and walking shoes had been stored out of sight, work schedules in front of us, we would very soon discard those thoughts as pipe dreams. The fridge magnets would rapidly be covered over with fliers for pizzas, dental appointment cards, daily task reminders lists. Here those dreams were floating on the surface, easy fish to reel in and trap in your net.

Around every corner you walked into a barrage of affirmations and positive thoughts engraved on trees, stones and walls. A last-minute crash diet of food for the soul. I stopped and gorged on them until I could not fit any more in. I was being constantly distracted from the very thing that they were urging me to do: to "be here now", "just walk", "dwell deeply in the present moment" and "feel truly alive". Sort of ironic. I allowed myself to consume one last tasty morsel: "Let's walk with the sun till our shadows disappear". So, I did. I turned my face away from all those clamouring thoughts and towards the sun. And just walked. Eventually even my Duracell batteries started to wear down. Nearing the town of O Pedrouzo, I sat in a field hidden by a hedge from the throng of passing humanity. I closed my eyes and listened to the crunching of stones under the passing feet. I tuned into snatches of birdsong in the brief instants of silence between and behind the steady thrum of chatter. Every now and then I would overhear intriguing snatches of intimate conversations; 'so will you keep it?' being the one that almost had me leap up from behind the hedge and run after them, desperately curious to know the identity of 'it'. A dress? An engagement ring?? A baby???

Eventually the only footsteps I was truly interested in hearing approached. I couldn't deny that my heart leapt a little as he looked up. We set off together falling seamlessly into step, on the search for the perfect lunch stop before getting the bus back to Arzua. Despite the crowds, we struck lucky and found a quiet, sun filled terrace, at a bit of a distance from the centre of town. Quiet being at a premium today.

We have all experienced that incomparable buzz of being focused exclusively on the person before us and receiving their undivided attention in return. Not really caring too much about our surroundings. But it sure did not hurt that here we were luxuriating in the essence of all things Camino. The low hum of contented conversation, the smell of seafood roasting in garlic infused olive oil wafting over us, our heads resting against the chair back tilted at just the right angle to feel the warmth of the sun, and the excitement of my hand just brushing his. Cruelly, the sun carried on its downward trajectory and the tables emptied around us. The last bus back to Arzua would soon be leaving town. So reluctantly, we got up to leave. I almost felt tempted to carve our initials in the tabletop. As we travelled eastwards rather than westwards, I silently willed the bus to keep on going all the way back to Irun. But no. It deposited us back in Arzua.

The distance to Santiago was now to be measured in hours. The final countdown had begun.

Chapter 27
SADLY SANTIAGO

"I think the thing is to enjoy the ride while you are on it."

Johnny Depp

O ver the years I had imagined walking into Santiago at the end of my first real Camino. I had imagined the deep significance I would feel with every step I took on that last day. I had never imagined taking a bus.

That bus would drop Andy, Celine, Diola and me at San Marcos, a spot just around the corner from the pilgrims' statues at Monte de Gozo on the outskirts of Santiago. We would then walk the impressive distance of 5 kms to the official end of the Camino. That 5 kms was the very most that Diola could manage. Ice and elevation had helped her foot. She was able to hobble. Every step of those last 5 kms would be deeply painful for her. There was no way in hell that Celine, Andy and I were going to let her walk that last 5 kms alone. So here we were in a cafe by the bus stop in Arzua, waiting to be driven into Santiago.

We were all slightly skittish, laughing and joking in a nervous, over caffeinated way. This day was deeply significant for each of us. All the little things we had done countless times before took on added gravitas and weight. This would be the last time we did them. The last time we packed our backpacks. The last time we decided how far to walk. The last time we all got a pre-walk coffee together. I tried to laugh and joke but I felt physically sick. I was driving myself crazy looking for significance in every word, every act and every thought. An older grey bearded pilgrim sat in the corner of the cafe. He looked deeply wise and spiritual. He was taking the bus too. So, it must be OK, I thought. I went over to see what words of wisdom he would dispense. But he was confused and disoriented. Muttering in broken English and German about broken dreams and broken bodies. Not exactly what I had been hoping for. I rejoined the others.

As I sat down, I noticed the sugar packets standing tall in their bright orange container. They were all stamped with a positive thought for the day. Was this where I would find my answer?

'Que las cosas no salgan como esperábamos muchas veces es lo mejor que nos puede pasar'

'When things don't turn out as we had expected, it is often the very best thing that could have happened to us.'

Ha! I wondered if the bar owner ordered that particular one in bulk to make us feel better. Let's face it, for any pilgrim getting the bus to Santiago, their Camino was probably not turning out how they had expected it to.

The bus dropped us off in San Marcos. We retrieved our packs from under the bus and merged with the slipstream of pilgrims headed to the Pope's statue. Everyone was focused on the end of their Camino. And so was I. I walked the same route I had taken many dozens of times over my years as a guide on the Gucci Camino. I compared each step to see if, this time, it felt different. I walked past the store where I always bought my bananas, past the statue where I always stopped and pressed my hand against its well-worn surface, and over there was the step where a client fell and broke both her ankles…. This was an uninvited and unhelpful dialogue playing in my head, constantly evaluating whether this time felt different…. Was this time imbued with deeper meaning? Was I seeing the world through new eyes? Was I was forever changed? Had the Camino transformed me? With so much bloody chatter in my head there was no available space for any possible answers to arise. I was unable to live the experience directly. The moment I had longed for, for so many years, was being stolen from me by my constant interrogation of myself.

Diola was hurting but fiercely determined. We had of course offered to take her pack and distribute the weight between us, but she wanted to carry it herself. We knew not to insist or mollycoddle her in any way, she would have hated that. She needed this moment under her own steam and on her own terms. Her last days had already been compromised enough by the pain she was in, this final part at least, had to take the shape she wanted.

Celine was buzzing around us like a nectar starved bee, talking non-stop, skipping alongside us, looking for some sort of reaction. Literally prodding and poking at us. Diola at first looked a little thunderous, she obviously wanted to be left in peace. She needed every bit of her strength, both inner and outer, to focus on her goal. I stepped in and engaged with Celine then let her spin off down the path.

We all strung out a bit but not for long.

We regrouped at a coffee stop, surreptitiously checking that Diola was OK. She had relaxed into Celine's behaviour. She got that Celine was simply unable to contain herself and her emotions. We walked more closely together, our little group forming and reforming in a fluid motion, all taking a moment with each other. As we turned a corner and could see the cathedral spires Celine's running commentary peaked in its excitement and Diola and I smiled at each other and rolled with it. She literally could not control herself. Andy hung back a bit observing the dynamics with a wry smile, understanding what was going on.

Before we entered the final strait into the cathedral square, we stood waiting for the lights to change so we could cross over the road to la Puerta del Camino. As we waited, I caught a glimpse of the many former versions of myself sitting in the front row seat of the cafe by those lights. I used to sit there scrutinising each and every passing pilgrim, wanting to know how and what they were feeling. What had the Camino revealed to them? What had they learned? I looked back at her as the lights changed. I just shrugged my shoulders in her direction, and I crossed the road. I had no concrete answers to give her about me.

Up past the fountain we went. We always told our Gucci Camino groups that the fountain's edges were worn down where horses had rested their heads to drink. I now wondered if that was true. Down past the jewellery shop selling the best silver and jet necklaces. I always recommended this shop to my groups. And finally, under the arch, where the lone bagpiper usually, but not always stood. I had always wondered if he would show up for the end of my Camino. Would he set the soundtrack to my final steps into the cathedral square? And there he was. Standing in the archway, where he always stood. Playing as I turned to walk down the stairs just before I caught my first glimpse of the cathedral.

We walked down those steps and into the square as a group, as we turned the corner, I found that my hand was in Andy's, or his in mine, certainly not a conscious decision it just happened. Then each of us naturally migrated to separate spots. There was no right way to do this. There was nothing that could have prepared us for this final footstep. For how this abrupt halt to all the forward momentum would feel. Like when the invigilator in your final exam tells you to put down your pen. All the worrying if you would be able to complete it, if you would give of your best, if you would express all you wanted to suddenly over, with a shocking finality that leaves you reeling. You could almost feel the spin of the earth as you put down your pen. Or your backpack. And looked up.

Even Andy was surprised to find himself having a full on moment.

Diola, despite, or maybe because of, it not having been the arrival she had envisaged was profoundly moved.

And Celine finally fell completely silent.

And as for me, I contemplated that facade.

I had taken it in a thousand times before. At last, I no longer had to ask how I felt, I knew. I just felt. All of it. The sadness, the joy, the relief, the fears, the elation, the guilt, the confusion, the enormity of it all. But above all, an overwhelming sense of joy and love and hope and trust. And deep gratitude. Without Diola, Andy and Celine I would not be here. I would have thrown in the towel. Run back to Granada to hide without ever having had this experience. There was that word that tripped me up on Gucci Camino. Experience. At last, I knew what it meant for me.

After we had had our individual moments, we regrouped in one massive hug. We didn't discuss how it had felt. I'm not sure there would have been sufficient words to do so. It was just between ourselves and Santiago. For me it was as if something had shifted inside me and for one blessed moment entirely shut down all of those clamouring thoughts. And just was, just felt, just 'be'd'. Not something that could be consciously conjured up or looked for. But I know we all experienced a version of this.

As we broke out of our hug, we saw Sarah and Richard windmilling at us from the other side of the square. We met them in the centre. Another mass embrace. They had been waiting for us. They had seen us walk in but had hung back to let us have our moments, knowing what we were experiencing, or at least their version of it. They said it had felt equally momentous to them.

Finally, my own 'real' photo in the cathedral square. Arms flung wide in triumph. All those times I had wondered what the pilgrims were feeling when they had their photos taken. Was it really as amazing as it looked? Well now I knew. Amazing just does not cover it. Amazing fell way short of my experience. Turned out that sugar packet philosopher had been spot on. This really had been the very best thing that could have happened to me. For so long I had been worried that this moment could not possibly live up to my inflated expectations of it. But it did. It exceeded them all.

Chapter 28
THE LAST SUPPER

"Don't cry because it's over. Smile because it happened."

Dr Seuss

I found the ideal bar for our last dinner together. There were barrels outside, old and worn. They served a functional, not decorative, role. Overflowing ashtrays were their only adornment. I peered through the dark and grimy window. This was obviously a no frills establishment. I could just make out scuffed low wooden tables that were jostling for space with benches for seating. Evidently the patrons here were all so familiar with each other they didn't care about sitting practically on top of each other. There were no opening times posted and no menu. No need. Those that frequented this place knew when to come and they knew the menu by heart. Here there would definitely be no pilgrims' menu on offer.

We all piled in. We weren't exactly welcomed with open arms but once they could see that we weren't the demanding, entitled breed of pilgrim they relaxed and accepted us. We happily crammed in tightly around a table. We were physically touching, having to clamber over each other when we needed to get up. And the food was outstanding. We feasted on calamares, ham, local soft cheese with anchovies, scrambled eggs with prawns, and my favourite; salmon in a creamy port-based sauce. All served with squat, square bottles of local Albariño wine. It was the perfect place for our last supper. Well, our last supper out together as a family. And it did seem Biblical in its importance. For all of us this had been an epic journey. I looked about me at the faces; faces that I had only known for a matter of weeks. Each face had become so very, very dear to me. I was flooded with so many emotions. I felt those emotions must be steaming off me in clouds visible to the eye. I was so overcome with it all, I excused myself to 'go to the loo', but instead I went and stood in the dark alleyway outside, standing just to one side of the window so they couldn't see me.

I watched them, in awe. It was hard to believe that just a few weeks ago I had come so very, very close to walking away from them all. I could see Diola's tall frame bent over to reach down to the table, suddenly throwing her head back in a belly laugh, no doubt at some quip Andy had made. Richard was at the end of the table, quiet and, as ever, unobtrusive. He was smiling and seemed content. He was never one to fully inhabit the present, too restless for that, he was probably planning his next big adventure. Sarah, on the other hand, was full of vitality and vigour, fully engaged with each and every one at the table. Celine was distributing thoughtful little Camino related gifts to everyone, her eyes sparkling with fun and warmth. And Andy, at the heart of the group, was entertaining everyone to the last. These people had taken me into their midst unquestioningly, supported me, accepted me, had seen me for all that I am and loved me for it, not despite it, as I had always secretly feared was the case with others. When I had been at my very lowest point ever, my most lost, they had been there for me to lift me up and show me the way. They had not only got me through, but they had also changed the course of my life. They had shown me that I was capable of moving through this world by myself. That I was enough. Just as I was.

Even though I had only known them for a number of weeks the depth of our sharing, the intensity of what we had been through belied this. Some experiences are impossible to measure in terms of linear time. What I lived and experienced in one Camino day was going to reverberate through my lifetime. Camino time defies the man-made construct of hours and minutes. These people had left an indelible imprint on my life, on my mind, heart and soul. Now I had to say goodbye to them. I hate goodbyes. At least I wasn't the one walking away from them. I couldn't do it. They were the ones who would be walking away from me. I took a deep, deep breath and went back inside. I squeezed back into my place among my Camino family.

Once we were back at the Airbnb flat, I couldn't bear it any longer. I couldn't pretend that this was just one more night all together on the Camino. The only thing for it was for me to get well and truly hammered. Having the tolerance level of a gnat where alcohol is concerned, three glasses of wine being my absolute upper limit, I achieved this easily. I have no recollection of actually going to bed, the next thing I remember is making an ungainly dash for the bathroom. Then lying cold and thoroughly miserable, naked on the bathroom floor with my arms wrapped around the great white telephone. I barely had enough strength to lift my head. I heard a knocking on the door and Andy asking if I was OK. "Don't come in!" I barked. I most definitely did not need him to see me like this. The knocking persisted.

"C'mon let me in, I've raised four teenage kids, nothing I haven't dealt with before". No way in hell was I letting him in. But the door opened. I evidently hadn't locked it. And he grabbed a large fluffy bath sheet and draped it around me. Then gently pulled my hair back from my face and stroked my back as I miserably leant time and again over the loo. It was the most romantic things anyone has ever done for me.

There was no stopping the goodbyes. The first was Celine. She had organised a car share ride back home to France. Again, I had to admire her style. She had got the car share guy to come through the winding streets of the old centre of Santiago to pick her up. No waiting at a main road bus stop for her. When she was all packed up she had one last typical Celine gesture to impose on us. Before Andy and Richard knew what was happening, she had us all holding hands in a prayer circle. At her command we closed our eyes. I squeezed tightly the hands in mine as she let rip with a prayer of love and appreciation for our Camino family and our Camino journey. Richard and Andy could barely believe that they had partaken in such a thing. Good old Celine. I was so grateful to her for this touching gift to us all. We ushered her out to her waiting car and waved her goodbye.

 One goodbye down. Five to go.

Sarah and Richard were next. They were going cycling in Portugal. No prayer circle for them. There were loving bear hugs all round from Sarah and manly one-armed hugs and slaps on the back from Richard. They promised to stay in touch so we could do this all again. Sarah gave us each a friendship bracelet and then they were off cycling down the road, southward bound for Portugal.

Three down. Three to go.

Next was Diola. She was flying home to Germany. Andy and I accompanied her to the airport. Before we got to her departure gate, she took me aside to ask me about my intentions towards Andy. She was very stern, like a Victorian father asking a suitor of his intentions towards his daughter. I told her that I honestly had no idea what, if anything would come of us, that I was very much my priority now and was not rushing into any sort of commitment. She understood that, but she wanted to make it very clear to me that any woman would be extremely lucky to be with a man like Andy. The Diola seal of approval was worth a very great deal to me. At the gate I reached up and she reached down for a massive heartfelt hug. This proud, beautiful, independent woman had taught me so much.

And then there were two. Andy and me.

It was our last night together on the Camino. We sat unobtrusively in the corner of our new local, the tiny bar where we had had dinner with the others. No hovering waiters or bright lights to distract us from each other. We kept it light and fun, reminiscing about our many reccys together when we had thought we were keeping 'us' secret from the others. How much fun it had been. We didn't allow ourselves to go 'there', to talk about the future. We focused on the wonderful food and the rustic atmosphere of the place. Andy would very shortly be back in grey and gloomy England. He needed to stockpile some Spanish warmth. We made our way through the hauntingly beautiful centre of Santiago. Its medieval streets steeped in a million tales of love, loss, heartache, romance, tragedy and comedy. Each and every facet of the human condition had been played out here. As we crossed the cathedral square, I became aware of a pink light softly illuminating the buildings. I rubbed my eyes, but the pink glow was growing deeper.

I looked at Andy. He was uncharacteristically quiet. He was aware of it too and was, for once, lost for words. As we went up the stairs from the cathedral where the lone bagpiper usually stood, there was an opera singer with a voice of such angelic purity and clarity that he didn't seem human. I couldn't help thinking that this would make for a great ending to a romantic movie. It was only later that I found out that we had been walking under the biggest, pinkest harvest moon the city had ever experienced.

And then I had to say goodbye to Andy. It was at the airport the very next day. Andy had to release himself from our final hug. I stood transfixed, unable to move. I watched him heft his pack on his back and turn and walk away from me. In true lone cowboy style, he disappeared. My mind knew that it was now time for me to move but my feet were not cooperating. Maybe I would become a permanent fixture at the departure gate. Maybe pilgrims would leave stones and mementoes at my feet. A statue, a shrine to Camino goodbyes. Eventually the security guards started to worry about me. They looked at me oddly. Should they move me on? That's not good, I thought. I needed to pull myself together. Through a superhuman force of will I walked myself out of the airport doors. I boarded the airport bus and headed back to Santiago. No more Camino family.

Now there was one. Just me. Alone. Now I had to say goodbye to the Camino.

I walked to the train station. I was ready to get the train back to Granada. To say the last goodbye, to the Camino. I was attending a wedding in Madrid in just over a week. Plenty of time to go home and get organised. At the ticket counter the clerk harrumphed impatiently.

Evidently, I had not yet told him my destination. Apparently, as I was no longer following the Camino script, I was unsure of my lines. "A donde va?' he eventually prompted me. "No lo sé" I found myself answering. Well that sure had not been in any script. I'd said that I didn't know. He suggested that I get out of the way and come back when I did. OK. Good. Someone was telling me what I should do. So, I got out the way. And started walking back to the cathedral square. And I walked and walked and walked. That I could do. I wasn't sure if I was ready to head back home to Granada. But if not Granada, then where? Finisterre occurred to me. Finisterre is the alternative final destination for many a pilgrim's Camino. It is a further 90 kms walk from Santiago. Finisterre means the end of the world. I had never walked to the end of the world before. It felt sort of tempting. But then it occurred to me that Pedro might have gone there. I did not want to walk with the thought that I could bump into him at any time. I walked aimlessly for a few more hours. And my thoughts followed the same circular route. Bouncing around between Granada and Finsterre. I headed back to the station. And stood in line. It was the same ticket clerk and he recognised me. "So do you know now?' He inquired in a tetchy fashion. I didn't dare tell him I still didn't know. A name. Just give him a place name. Now. And what came out of my mouth was 'Santander'. Huh?! Well, that was news to me. But I knew that was right. That was indeed where I wanted to go. I wasn't ready for that last goodbye yet. I was going to complete my incomplete Camino. I had missed walking the section from Santander to Villaviciosa. I'd jumped it when I went to my work conference in Sarajevo a lifetime ago. It wasn't about the distance or the places I had missed, it was about celebrating myself. I was going to go and walk on my own. I was going to test my ability to be alone but not lonely. To go and do entirely what I wanted to do with no one else around to please. The clerk handed me my ticket.

Just me n' Boris out on the road.

Chapter 29
AND THEN THERE WAS ONE

"Always look for the light, for it is always looking for you!"

David Strickel

"Walk as if you are enough. Eat as if you are enough. See, look, listen as if you are enough. Because it's true."

- Geneen Roth.

My train arrived late into Santander where I had booked myself into a hostal. My plan was to get some provisions and eat in my room. I headed out to the supermarket. As I walked past bars full of light and laughter the thought of eating in my room no longer seemed appealing. I had never eaten dinner out at a restaurant on my own before. That seemed nuts! About bloody time I did then, I thought. I checked out a menu posted on a window. It looked good. So, I went in. I felt shy and vulnerable as if I had an arrow over my head with the words 'Loser! Table for one for this sad lonely woman!' written on it. I slunk to a corner table. The conversations at the other tables hadn't stopped. No one was looking over at me. I resisted the urged to bury my head in my phone or call someone to keep me company. I sat and people watched. I enjoyed the very Spanishness of the experience. Even after all these years of living in Spain, it never failed to thrill me. I loved the understated ceremony. All the diners greeted the tables already seated, wishing them a good meal. The waiters were gruff but highly professional. As I watched, it occurred to me that waiting tables is a respected profession in Spain not something unemployed actors and students do half-heartedly to earn their keep. My solo dining experience was a pleasure. I swaggered out of the restaurant and back to my room. You would have thought I had just climbed Everest. Well, I sort of had. My own private summit of dinner for one.

The next morning, I was so excited to get on the Camino I set off absurdly early. I took a local train. Eschewing the grimy industrial outskirts of Santander. I only had to go a few stops to a village from where I could hook up with the Camino. The train's regulars were already immersed in their busy day ahead, laptops out, talking on their phones, fully engaged with flow charts, presentations, productivity goals. I was the only person not suited and booted for a day at the office. I stepped off the train into the pitch black pre-dawn, with no clue as to where I should be headed, and no one awake yet to ask. I bumbled around to the outskirts of the village, flagged down a passing car and was pointed in the right direction. The sense of relief and joy on seeing my first yellow arrow was huge. I stopped and hugged the tree on which it was painted. It seemed as surprised as I was. Celine would be proud of me.

Finally, I was walking on my own. No Gucci Camino tour to nurture, no husband to consider and no Camino family looking out for me. On my own. Just me n' Boris back on the path. I felt uneasy. I had an uncomfortable feeling that I could not shake off. I tried to talk myself out of it. I reminded myself that if I had followed my original plan, I would now be in Granada washing my hiking gear, stowing Boris away, and back in my daily grind. It didn't work. The unease was still with me. I needed something to distract me. I plugged in my headphones. This was something I didn't often do while I walked. I tuned into an early morning English radio programme. It was light and uplifting, guests with interesting stories. A chef was describing mouth-watering delights, which made me realise I was famished. I hadn't even had coffee yet. There was nowhere open this early on a Saturday morning. I shot them an email saying where I was and asked them to stop torturing me with their talk of food. They read it out on air, and I immediately received a WhatsApp from my sister Penny. She was listening to the same radio show. She asked how I was doing. I hadn't been in touch with her since our initial chats in early September at the beginning of my Camino. It was good to reconnect with her. She tentatively mentioned that Mum had been asking about me. Maybe I could give her a call?

What really surprised me about this strange coincidence was not that Penny and I were listening to the same radio programme but that I really wanted to talk to my mum. I never called her out of the blue unless it was her birthday or Christmas. I rang her. She answered immediately. I found myself telling her all about Pedro leaving me. She was unconditionally supportive and loving, exactly as I had always wanted her to be as I was growing up. I didn't self-edit. I wasn't the perky positive character I thought she wanted me to be. I even swore for the first time ever in her presence. There was a bit of a stunned silence from both of us. She broke the silence by agreeing with me that, yes, it had all been f…ing hard. I had never heard my mum say anything stronger than 'gosh' before. We had a heartfelt, meaningful and deeply comforting conversation. So much better than our usual obligatory awkward calls. I felt cherished and loved. I had let my mum mother me.

Immediately my discomfort left. I felt rejuvenated. 'Ain't no stopping us now' I sang to Boris as we motored along. I sighted my first other pilgrim. He was on another path. Friendly chap, waving enthusiastically at me. I waved back. He waved harder. Seemed a little odd, such enthusiasm. Once again, I waved back. The waving became more energetic, sticks were windmilling above his head. Finally, it dawned on me that he needed my help. Maybe he was lost or hurt. I had better go see. I trotted on up to him. "It's this way" were his first words. While I was talking to mum, I had missed an arrow and veered off the Camino. So much for my superior arrow detection skills. I was so thankful to this pilgrim for getting me out of trouble.

Having left so early and having moved at quite a clip, I was the first pilgrim to arrive in the small "town" of Caborredondo, population 20. When I signed in at the albergue it gave me a thrill to look back through the register and see the names of my Camino family. The memories of their warmth and love came flooding back to me. I took myself off for a little trot around town. I was really hungry now. There was no shop, the closest being 10 kms away. I had already walked 40 kms, so I was going to have to tough it out until dinner. I had a brief glimmer of hope when I found a vending machine, but it sold only condoms, fizzy drinks and chocolate bars that were full up with gluten. It would be a long wait until the only bar opened at 8.00pm. I lay on my back in a field next to the albergue. I communed with the gorgeous doe eyed cows. They munched contentedly around me. The only sounds were the clanging of their huge copper bells and the rumblings of my stomach.

When I headed back to the albergue a Camino family had taken over the kitchen and communal area. They were organised. They had arrived with their own provisions to make dinner. I sat and chatted for a bit. It felt odd to see another group of pilgrims bonded with contentedness and unity like mine had been. They were friendly but I could tell they didn't want an outsider disturbing their group dynamic. That was fine by me. I was looking forward to repeating my lone dining experience. When the bar doors opened at 8.00pm I practically trampled the poor guy in my rush to get my order in for tortilla and salad. I could see they were used to hungry pilgrims. Still, I think they were a little taken aback at the ravenous glint in my eye.

Having a condensed time frame in which to walk and seeing each step as a bonus heightened my sense of appreciation for it all. As these days continued, I had an ever growing sense of confidence in my ability to be alone. I didn't latch on to the first pilgrims to cross my path. I was friendly and open. But I always made it clear that I was happy walking alone. On the Camino there is always the option to have company unlike in everyday life where if you walked up to a total stranger and asked if you could accompany them, they would run very fast in the opposite direction. The days were shorter now. In the mornings I stumbled around in the dark until that pre-dawn pause when even the birds and the shimmering trees seem to be holding their breath in a communal moment of magic. And then I would walk on into another Camino sunrise. Leaving a village called Poo - of course I had to stay there, how could I not? - I obediently followed the pale yellow arrows that were slowly becoming more vibrant as the dimmer switch on dawn was gradually being dialled up a few notches. The privilege of being there floored me. I was so mesmerised by the gaudily painted sky, like a small child had applied her mother's make up with huge slashes of garish red lipstick, that I almost didn't notice that the arrows had pointed me to the very edge of a cliff. One more step and my Camino would have come to an abrupt close, very like Thelma & Louise.

In the depths of Boris, I had found a blue woollen hat with a note attached. A present from Andy. He had bought it for me in Santiago and secretly hidden it there as a surprise. I was certainly grateful for it. It was getting noticeably chillier. The streams I crossed weren't tinkling underfoot but burping and gurgling like an overfull bathtub you'd pulled the plug on. I was no longer jumping into piles of crunchy leaves but wading through claggy mounds of them like pushing your spoon through soggy cornflakes. Button mushrooms sprouted like dropped pennies all over the path. In the field huge pumpkins lay on their backs, like bloated beached whales.

In Ribadesella, I stayed in a repurposed mansion that served as a smart surf school, that in turn served as an albergue. We pilgrims went to sleep lulled by the same sounds of the ocean as those who had paid full whack for this privilege. I woke during the night momentarily wondering what the noise was, then lay back willing myself to stay awake to float arms and legs outstretched like a starfish in my bunk. Luxuriating in the feeling of being buoyed by my friend the sea. I was being gently breathed in and out by the rise and fall of the waves but was all too soon pulled back under by the soothing womb like sounds.

I was up first before the other pilgrims. I made us all coffee in the scullery like kitchen and brought it up to the dorm. There were only a few of us there. There was a very tall, very quiet, shy Canadian. Probably in his late 60's. He seemed astonished but pleased to have someone bring him coffee. I could sense he was one of my former tribe of sad solo walkers. I silently wished him well. I trusted the Camino to work its magic on him. But I knew he most definitely did not want to be told that. I left them to their coffee and set out into another bright but chilly day, happy in my new blue hat, wishing the shy Canadian and the others a "Buen Camino".

I was passing very few people now. In late October on the Norte albergues were starting to close down and pilgrims were becoming a rare breed. I was heading into Villaviciosa. I would be revisiting the scene of the crime. Where my Camino family had come precariously close to splintering. And the place where I had spent my last lonely night sharing a bed with Pedro. I was looking forward to striding back through there victorious. But the nearer I got, the worse I felt. For the first time since I had been walking alone, I felt a sense of real panic. What would I do if I fell to pieces? Who would be there to pick me up? There was no Diola or Celine or Andy. Would I be able to get myself back up on my feet? I was trembling both within and without. The only thing that kept me going was "The Camino doesn't give you what you want but what you need." I had so much first-hand experience of this already. I held on tight and tried to stop myself shattering into a myriad pieces. I found a field where I could sit unobserved and just let the sadness have its way with me. I now realised it was part of why I had needed to walk this section alone. It was part of my healing. I gave into the wisdom of the Camino and let myself shatter. After the tempest had done its worst and I started to come back into myself. I sat quietly and marvelled that I had survived it alone. I did not need anyone to rescue me. What I did need now was a very large cafe con leche to soothe and fortify me. I made my way past the hostal where we had stayed and crossed the road to the cafe filled with memories of my Camino family.

The unmistakable long legs of the Canadian protruded from under the same outdoor table that my Camino family had sat at. He was bent awkwardly to one side so as not to obstruct the path of the good people of Vicious Town. I was really, really pleased to see him. He could, of course, tell that I had just had a sob fest. I could hardly conceal it. He didn't pass comment, just ordered me a cafe con leche and let me take my time. We sat in companionable silence. It was soothing to sit there in the company of another who understood sadness. Eventually I looked up and could read the invitation to talk if that was what I wanted. And I did. I shared my story. And in the sharing, I felt myself returning, the shattered self that had been lying in wait for me here was shrinking as the brightness of my mood increased in the warmth of this stranger. Then this kind and gentle man told me that I reminded him of his daughter of whom he was extremely proud. He spoke of the qualities he perceived in us both. He said he knew that my father would be very proud of me too. All my life the kid within me had wanted to hear this. He then honoured me by sharing a little of his reason for being on the Camino. Which was as I had known, deeply personal and deeply sad. We were two strangers just listening to each other's stories. I can only hope that in the sharing, his shattered self also faded a little.

The final night came. I spent it at the same campsite outside Gijon that we had stayed at before. A small group of pilgrims including my friend, the Canadian, were there and we shared a peaceful and happy dinner together. My last night on the Camino. No fanfare, no huge celebration, no need for bells and whistles. We sat outside together sharing a glass of wine, stories, and the stars.

The next morning, I said goodbye to my gentle friend and took my final Camino walk into Gijon. At the train station I walked past a man holding the hand of a tiny boy. They looked like father and son. The man crouched down next to the little boy and pointed towards me. I heard him telling his son that I was a 'pergrina'. Wow. I hadn't expected that. There was my proof that I was at last one of them, a pilgrim. And I was proud to be playing my tiny part in the ever-evolving Camino story that was such an integral piece of their culture and heritage.

I continued to the ticket office. The clerk looked up at me. But before he could even get out "A donde va?" I requested a one way ticket to Madrid. And Boris and I stepped on to the train.

EPILOGUE

It's now 2022. Almost five years on from my Camino.

And I'm still married to Pedro.

And still sleeping with Andy.

No, we're not in some modern polygamous relationship. I just haven't got round to getting divorced yet. Keep meaning to but something more interesting always gets my attention.

It is often said that your Camino only really starts when you get to Santiago. That might be a bit of a cliche, but for me that has proved to be true. Those seeds of self-love and self-worth had been planted in what was pretty shallow soil back then. They've taken root and flourished since. I have dug deeper and weeded out all those past experiences I once let define me. In the light of acceptance and forgiveness, they've naturally withered and made room for far healthier more sustaining growth.

The appreciation I feel for all that I experienced on the Camino, and for those with whom those experiences unfolded has likewise grown enormously. I am quite literally in awe at the power of that pathway across northern Spain and its alchemical effect on those fortunate enough to walk it. With their hearts and minds open.

Once I stopped running away from myself and faced the deepest darkest corners of my past, I found that the fear of what I might encounter was far greater than actually facing those demons. I've come to appreciate all that has led me to where I am now. Understanding very deeply that life is always happening for me, not to me. Fear had made my life small and constricted. The relief and joy of no longer living my life to please others for their approval is immense.

For the generosity of spirit and unconditional support I received from my Camino family I shall never be able to find words sufficient to express my gratitude. Had it not been for them, my Camino would have come to a crashing halt in that beige room in Gijon, and God knows where I would be today. I shudder to even contemplate that.

After the Camino, I returned to my little cave home in Granada and loved living there alone. Andy and I started up what became a daily conversation over morning coffee, just like on the Camino, only via WhatsApp rather than in person. I then walked the Camino Portuguese coastal route with him in May of the following year. And we've been together since then. Sarah and Richard came and visited my cave home. I'm still in touch with Diola and Celine. Andy still threatens to go round to Diola's place and mess up her cushions one day.

To anyone even just contemplating walking the Camino, particularly if you're feeling stuck in any way, I would say grab your walking shoes and go. In my opinion, the chances of your regretting doing so are practically non-existent, whilst the chances that you will regret not doing it are immense. To give yourself the opportunity of, as per Andy, walking back into your own arms is, to my mind, the greatest gift you could give yourself. And as Rumi said, we are all just walking each other home. Nowhere could that feel truer than on the Camino.

THE END

Made in United States
North Haven, CT
28 March 2023

34642381R10135